YOU CAN KNOW GOD

Christian Spirituality for Daily Living

MARILYN GUSTIN

LIGUORI
PUBLICATIONS

ONE LIGUORI DRIVE
LIGUORI, MO 63057-9999
(314) 464-250'

D1367769

Imprimi Potest:
James Shea, C.SS.R.
Provincial, St. Louis Province
The Redemptorists

Imprimatur:
Monsignor Maurice F. Byrne
Vice Chancellor, Archdiocese of St. Louis

ISBN 0-89243-479-1
Library of Congress Catalog Card Number: 92-74594

Copyright © 1993, Liguori Publications
Printed in U.S.A.

Scripture selections taken from THE NEW AMERICAN BIBLE WITH THE REVISED NEW TESTAMENT, copyright © 1986, AND THE REVISED PSALMS, copyright © 1991, by the Confraternity of Christian Doctrine, Washington, D.C., and are used with permission. All rights reserved.

Excerpts from the English translation of *The Roman Missal,* copyright © 1973, International Committee on English in the Liturgy (ICEL), are used with permission. All rights reserved.

Excerpts from *Angelus Silesius: The Cherubinic Wanderer,* translated by Maria Shrady, copyright © 1986; *Bernard of Clairvaux,* translated by G. R. Evans, copyright © 1987; *Birgitta of Sweden,* edited by Marguerite Tjader Harris, copyright © 1990; *Bonaventure,* translated by Ewert Cousins, copyright © 1978; *Catherine of Siena: The Dialogue,* translated by Suzanne Noffke, OP, copyright © 1980; *Maximus the Confessor,* translated by George C. Berthold, copyright © 1985; *Meister Eckhart: The Essential Sermons, Commentaries, Treatises and Defense,* translated by Edmund Colledge, OSA, and Bernard McGinn, copyright © 1981; *Symeon the New Theologian: The Discourses,* translated by C. J. deCatanzaro, copyright © 1980; Gregory of Nyssa, *The Life of Moses,* translated by Abraham Malherbe and Everett Ferguson, copyright © 1978; *Julian of Norwich,* Grace M. Jantzen, copyright © 1988, The Society for Promoting Christian Knowledge (SPCK), London, England; Paulist Press, New York, New York, are used with permission.

Excerpts from *The Cloud of Unknowing,* edited by William Johnston, copyright © 1973; *Desert Wisdom,* Yushi Nomura, copyright © 1982, Doubleday, Dell Publishing Group, Inc., Garden City, New York, are used with permission.

Excerpts from *Evagrius Ponticus: The Praktikos and Chapters on Prayer,* translated by John Eudes Bamberger, O.C.S.O., copyright © 1978; *Sayings of the Desert Fathers,* translated by Benedicta Ward, SLG, copyright © 1978, Cistercian Publications, Kalamazoo, Michigan, are used with permission.

Excerpts from *Illuminations of Hildegard of Bingen,* Matthew Fox, copyright © 1985; *Hildegard's Scivias,* edited by Bruce Hozeski, copyright © 1986; Bear and Company, Santa Fe, New Mexico, are used with permission.

Excerpts from *Meister Eckhart,* translated by Raymond B. Blakney, copyright © 1941, Harper and Row Publishers, Inc., New York, New York. Reprinted by permission of HarperCollins Publishers.

Excerpts from *The Philokalia,* Volume Two, translated and edited by G.E.H. Palmer, Philip Sherrard, and Kallistos Ware, copyright © 1986, Faber and Faber, Inc., Winchester, Massachusetts, are used with permission.

Cover design by Pam Hummelsheim

Dedication

For John
Beloved husband,
best friend

Contents

Prologue

But why am I, a poor person, running about the two higher heavens with my tongue, talking with more loquacity than spiritual liveliness, when with my hands and feet I am still striving down here? At his bidding and with his help I have put up a ladder for myself....

But I climb slowly, a weary traveler, and I need somewhere to rest. Woe is me if the darkness surrounds me...for now, even at an acceptable time...I can scarcely make my way.

Why am I so slow? Pray for me anyone who is my son, brother, friend, companion of my journey in the Lord. Pray for me to the Almighty, that he may give my footsteps vigor and that the foot of pride may not come near me. For a weary foot is no use in climbing to the truth.

...for I can make no progress in my own strength....I, too, Lord, will freely glory if I can, in my weakness...so that your strength...may be perfected.[1]

Bernard of Clairvaux
1090-1153

Introduction

T he urgency of his question haunted me. For many months I debated with myself whether yet another book about spirituality should be written. In the end, permission came through prayer, but I might have forgotten the project long ago had it not been for naval Commander Dick Heames. He was a student in a graduate class I taught in Christian spirituality. He is also a husband, the father of eight children, and devoted to his parish and community.

Though his exact words are lost to memory now, his intensity grips me still:

"But what about us? When I've been at sea for six months, there's only one thing on my mind when I get home. When I'm home enjoying my wife, surrounded by kids, my time jammed with church and community commitments, when I'm worried about the way the world is going—how can I find God? I long for God sometimes, but for me there will never be a monastery or anything nearly like it. All the models ever held up to me have been celibate and institutionalized. What about me? Is there no possibility for me to know God?"

The same cry arises silently in many hearts. It is a cry that for years lived passionately, nearly desperately—sometimes angrily—in my own heart. Perhaps that is why I've been so compelled by Dick and his counterparts, women and men, who ache for God and say so but who don't know how to begin a deeper search. By God's incredible grace, help has been granted me. I want to share it. If you are homesick for God, this book is written for you.

So to all of you who wonder if you can live in God's heart in this ordinary, busy life of yours…

You CAN Know God

Y es.

Yes, you can experience God right where you are. Yes, you can know the Lord more and more directly in your ordinary life. Your home, your family, your friends, your work—in the very midst of all this, your usual life—God is available to you. You *can* know God.

A thousand years ago, Saint Symeon the New Theologian said it well:

> Some praise life in a desert, others life in monasteries, still others a place of authority among people, to instruct and teach them and organize churches where many may find food for body and soul. I would not wish to give preference to any of these, nor to say that one is worthy of praise and another of censure. In all ways of life, blessed is the life lived for God and according to God in all actions and works.[1]

You do not have to go off to—anywhere. You do not have to be a priest, a nun, or a monk. Union with God is not restricted to particular situations, although circumstances can help or hinder the process.

Union with God happens in our heart, in our own innermost self. What matters is what we do within ourselves exactly where we are.

Then why, you may ask, do we have the examples we do? Someone asked Meister Eckhart a similar question. He replied, "Our Lord gave them this manner of life, and he also gave them the strength to act like that....But God has not made human salvation depend on any such particular way of life. What is peculiar to one way of life is not found in another; but it is God who has endowed all holy practices with the power of fulfillment, and it is denied to no good way of life."[2]

To know God, to move increasingly toward oneness with God, is our birthright as Christians. The journey toward transforming union with God is precisely Jesus Christ's invitation to each of us. "Oh, sure," you may say, "I know I can see God in heaven and live with him there." Yes, that too. But what we often do not know—or ignore—is that God can be known, "seen," experienced, loved, entirely in this present earthly life of ours. The writers of Scripture knew that. The Psalmist sings: "Return, my soul, to your rest; the LORD has been good to you....I shall walk before the LORD in the land of the living" (Psalm 116:7, 9).

Furthermore, Jesus' teaching is filled with the message that God is for us *now*. He called it "the kingdom of God," or "the reign of God," implying that God is fully in charge of our living and that we live in him. Yet for most Christians, that remains a mere ideal rather than a living experience. The kingdom is at hand, Jesus urged us, right here, among you, within you! His teaching aimed to entice us to open ourselves to God now and here, not later, not somewhere else.

Over and over, especially in John's Gospel, Jesus tells his followers that he wants them to be one with him just as he is one with the Father, so we can all be one. That is union, full oneness. Union with God is what Jesus Christ wanted for his disciples—and still wants. Jesus came to tell us that, to show us that. He came to set us on the pathway to the Father and to do anything necessary to make it possible for each of us who wish it.

Do you experience God fully and steadily right now? If you have picked up this book, probably not. But somewhere within our being, we long for God. God has touched each of us with his "personal" invitation to come to full life in his heart. We may know that. We may know that certain experiences, certain inner aches or hungers, are God's allurements. If you recognize his invitations in your own life, the next few paragraphs may not tell you anything new. But if you are not at all sure God has touched you or invited you to anything in particular, please consider the following examples.

Someone walks in the woods, the desert, or along a beach. Suddenly, there is a feeling of openness, a heightened awareness of the surroundings. Everything seems to be of a piece, interconnected, including the person. Have you been that person?

Someone is gripped by periodic homesickness, a nameless nostalgia for—something. That something may be elusive, unidentifiable; but the emotion is clearly recognizable. It is not especially pleasant, and it may actually be painful. It can appear in the midsection of the body at any time. It seems unrelated to external events, but it does seem to accompany a certain awareness of one's own inner being. If you have experienced this, you may have mistaken it for "something wrong with me," a neurosis or worse. But it isn't anything wrong. It is God inviting you to himself. You simply may not know how to recognize his touch.

Someone experiences a time of unreasonable peacefulness. Peace flows through the whole being without having been sought. It is there, within. The mind quiets itself, emotions fade, and silence arises inside. The whole being fills with serenity. Happenstance? No, God's touch. Wouldn't you like to be able to return to this experience, even to live in it all the time? It is possible.

A sudden encounter with beauty in art or a truthful idea can make one gasp with appreciation and wonder. Sudden tears may spring up from the heart. One wishes to take this beauty deeply within, to keep it forever. Then that moment fades in memory and is lost. Still, it is God, reminding you of his own beauty, calling you to accept more of himself.

The invitation may come as a deep rapport, an awareness of belonging to this place, this time, these people. A contented "ah" may arise in the heart. You may connect this feeling with outer circumstances, and indeed circumstances may trigger it. The circumstances only bear the love of God to us, however, welcoming us.

God may speak to you by causing you to feel restless, unsatisfied with things as they are. This restlessness is not just a matter of not having what you want but a chronic feeling of casting about looking for something more, something subtler, something lasting or somehow more true. Beliefs and circumstances do not still this restlessness. You may have tried this and that, looked here and there for the answer—in career or status or children or friends or even marriage. But restlessness of the heart, beyond circumstances, is God's invitation to come live in him, profoundly and consistently. The heart wants God.

Someone may experience sudden joy without apparent cause, welling up from somewhere deep within, unsought and unexpected, flowing like a fountain until she or he wishes never to live without it. Then it fades...

You may have thought that experiences like these were mere fleeting feelings, nice maybe—or maybe not—but without particular significance. You may have had much more profound experiences that have gone unexplained. You may have ignored them or been puzzled by them, even frightened.

If this is true for you, it may be that you do not know yet what a spiritual life, an interior life with God, can be. You may have thought that union with God is only for "specially called" saints who knew what they wanted almost from babyhood. You may even have been taught that wanting God, desiring oneness with the Lord, longing for the divine Presence in your heart—that all these were presumption and not meant for anyone as ordinary as you.

The truth is that our longing, even when half-hidden under the stimulation and stress of a busy life, is alive because God wants to give himself fully to us. It was for loving union with him that he created us. It is to union with him that he invites us by putting our longing so deep within us. It is also the primary reason the Son came to earth, took flesh, and lived among us.

The Mystical Tradition

If you are uncertain about God's invitation, you may have picked up a certain suspicion about mystics that has been prevalent in the Church since the Council of Trent. Thank God, because enough people now are clamoring for help, we are rediscovering our own mystical tradition and the guidance of the great Christian mystics.

What is a mystic? The word *mystic* has been much used and misused to mean some strange things: mysterious, supernatural, weird, nonunderstandable—or as one of my friends says, "Woooo-woooo-woooo!" In Christianity (and in this book), *mystic* refers to a person who has become one with God in divine union. That union is classically known as "mystical union," meaning the full oneness of a human being with the Holy Trinity. Because of this mystical union, such human beings are called "mystics" or sometimes "mystical saints."

A unifying, healing, joyful, and wondrous life with God is the very purpose of human creation. It is the purpose of Jesus' life and work and death and resurrection. If you feel a spark of recognition, a tiny flame of interest, it is the purpose of your life, even though you may not yet acknowledge it fully.

So, right in the beginning, let's acknowledge that our inner longing and other inner experiences are a great good. We do well to honor our own experience; it is, after all, the only one we have. God honors our experience by touching our heart through it. We are invited to pay attention. Not every valuable experience may seem positive. But our heart still hungers for God.

Some people know their hunger is for God but have no idea how to respond to it. Many have asked serious spiritual questions, only to be misunderstood or even rebuffed. Some have given up on Christianity because it did not seem to be recognizably profound enough for the spirit within or because it did not seem to offer definite direction. These seekers have looked elsewhere, and often they have found help elsewhere.

Chances are, though, you have told no one about these intimate, often fleeting, experiences simply because you have rarely heard of anyone else who has had similar experiences. For years I did not mention my experiences to a single soul; consequently, I failed to find the help or companionship I needed. If I asked for advice, my question was carefully couched in the "right" language. No one recognized the source of my longing, and that worried and frustrated me. I never expressed it straightforwardly.

Many people find support for their interior search only with great difficulty. Society, friends—even the Church—do not always provide guidance or understanding. Too many of us have asked a priest about spiritual life or how to know God fully, only to be told something vague or maybe discouraging. Nevertheless, if we recognize our own experience of God's invitation, we must trust it; it is the truest gift given to us. Then we must take initiative to help ourselves open more fully to that urgent, beautiful call.

God calls us all, each and every one, to a deep divine love, a constant and lasting peace, a full and dynamic joy.

God is a patient, determined lover. God constantly offers us himself in every way imaginable. He touches each heart precisely as it is likely to be able to receive the divine invitation. God is always giving himself, as fully and rapidly as we can receive. This is grace. It flows freely from the heart of God at every moment, never pausing, never ceasing. Mostly, we stand on the bank of this river of love and do not know how to plunge in. But take courage! We can learn to drink from this water of life, to be filled with it and to be fully immersed in it forever. Starting now.

Every single aspect of our life is potentially a place where we experience God because we are called to experience him first and always in our heart. Our heart is always with us, right in the middle of all our activities. If we really want results, we search for God within, where the Holy Spirit dwells. As we find the Spirit there, and learn to remain attentive and open to the holy Presence within, we may come to know God directly at the very same time we are "doing" our life.

"Wait a minute," you may say. "We have heard the theory of Christianity all our lives." Yes. In many of us, Christian *theory* has acted almost like a vaccination: a little of the vaccine has made us immune to the full "illness." That is, we may have thought that assenting to Christian beliefs was the whole of Christianity. That assumption has prevented us from opening to the full *experience* of God which Christianity essentially offers.

Belief and Experience

We easily forget that the first Christians had no theology. They had experience. Jesus Christ gave them an experience of life in the presence of God. Can you imagine Matthew, for example, jumping up from a profitable job to follow this unknown preacher unless something extraordinary had happened in his insides? His heart must have blown so wide open to this young roaming rabbi that he could not stay away. Certainly, no belief system in itself has that kind of power. Nobody stood before Matthew's tax table and explained Jesus as a member of the Trinity. No one gave Matthew a preachment telling him how he ought to live complete with rules. Only a shock of joy could send someone dashing after an unknown wanderer—or a blast of peace or love unimagined or a vision of freedom.

We twentieth-century Christians have the beliefs and the rules. We often do not have the experience the Church originally intended to support and to strengthen.

This lack need not be a matter for blame, however; the door to experiential spirituality is not completely shut. In the heart of the Christian tradition, we can still discover a vital stream that flows from the love of Christ experienced and known in this life. Bernard of Clairvaux often insists on experience, too. "The touch of the Holy Spirit teaches, and it is learned by experience alone. Let those who have experienced it enjoy it; let those who have not, burn with desire, not so much to know it as to experience it."[3]

I believe that Christianity is alive today because of its inner tradition of union with God, sought and found in experience by those who loved him, not because of institutional longevity or the political savvy of Church leaders through the centuries. If we long for God, our hope is to be found in those Christians, no matter when they lived, who knew God directly in their own heart and wrote about their life and experience. Through them, we may rediscover the vitality in Christianity for ourselves. Through them, with our own practical efforts and the continuing grace of God, we ourselves can come to live in the heart of God, now and always.

LEARNING FROM THE EXPERTS

We desire to live in God. We know that it is possible. But desire and knowledge are not enough. Once, in a group discussing spirituality, someone had the courage to ask flatly what all of us were wondering. "In *my* life? Balancing the checkbook, making love, battling teenagers, driving zillions of miles, working my tail off? If it's possible to know God in all of that, *tell me how!*"

We need to know how. We need to know how to begin, then how to continue.

If you want to be a concert violinist, you will naturally seek the best teacher you can find. A master violinist has practiced, experienced, and demonstrated what you want to learn. If you want to climb to the top of an unfamiliar mountain, you will hire a guide who knows every step of the path, starting at the bottom.

It is the same with the spiritual journey. It involves skills we do not have at the beginning. It takes us through unfamiliar territory. We need an expert—or several of them.

Why can't the Lord be our only guide? He can and has been for some. Yet even the greatest of Christians received counsel from others. The Lord will certainly guide us—and much of that guidance will come through other people. In the beginning, though, we simply don't know how to recognize clearly the Lord's guidance and distinguish it from the fertility of our own mind, our own ego.

Some of the best help is available from the writings of great Christians, men and women who experienced transforming mystical union with God and who taught and wrote about their interior life.

So it is to Christian mystics that we will turn in these pages. We will take their words for our pondering and our experimenting. We will explore their ideas and practices to find those we can use in our own efforts. We will ponder their attitudes toward God and toward themselves to see whether we can cultivate a similar stance of our own.

What we will *not* do is try to copy their lifestyle. In the first place, we live in the twentieth century and that alone makes a huge difference. More importantly, however, a lifestyle is external; it is behavior. It is not totally unrelated to inner life with God, but it is not the same thing. If we seek and find the inner spiritual life, our behavior and lifestyle will take care of themselves. Likewise, our external choices may or may not support our interior life. We'll try to discover how to know what helps us. So when we turn to the mystics, we will look for ways to imitate their aim and their intensity. We will seek "how to" tips, measuring each one to find what is most appropriate and helpful for us.

Most of these experts, though not all, were celibate. That does not mean celibacy is required. It may mean that people who did not have families had time to write about their inner life. Or it may mean that writings are better preserved within the Church's organization than outside it. For some who know how to use it, celibacy has been a wonderful support for interior effort. It has crippled others. So let's remember that spiritual life in its essence is an *interior* process. It expresses itself in many outward behavioral forms, and celibacy and marriage are both included in those forms.

One highly useful way to gather practical help from mystical writing is to look for the dynamics of spiritual life. How does a particular practice function in growth? How does it affect the person who practices it? What changes does it support? Would that same practice have that same function in our life? Perhaps. Perhaps not. We look, with as much prayerful discernment as we can muster, for the movements and changes that need to take place in us, however they happen, and we find ways of encouraging them in ourselves for God's sake. The mystics offer wonderful help with the search.

We will seek help from fourteen men and women who lived in various times from the third through the seventeenth centuries. Some of them will be familiar; others will likely be new to you. Their names and the dates of their lives are

Desert Fathers and Mothers: 250-425
Gregory of Nyssa: 335-395
Evagrius: 345-399
Maximus the Confessor: 580-662
Symeon the New Theologian: 949-1022
Hildegard of Bingen: 1098-1179
Bernard of Clairvaux: 1090-1153
Bonaventure: 1217-1274
Meister Eckhart: 1260-1327
Author of *The Cloud of Unknowing*:
    late fourteenth century
Birgitta of Sweden: 1302-1373
Catherine of Siena: 1347-1380
Julian of Norwich: 1342-(not before 1413, but uncertain)
Angelus Silesius: 1624-1677

In the Appendix, beginning on page 183, you will find a brief biography of each of these people. The Bibliography, beginning on page 211, lists the sources referred to in the notes at the end of each chapter as well as other sources I used for background in the mystics' biographies.

Why have these particular mystics been selected from the hundreds of possibilities? And why are no contemporaries included?

I cannot claim that these choices necessarily represent the greatest mystics. How could one make such a judgment? However, I chose them as guides for several reasons. First, they knew God directly in their own experience and wrote about it. Second, their writings have nourished countless Christians for hundreds of years. Third, I believe it is time we get to know our own tradition. Untold riches for our spiritual development lie with the Christian mystics of the past, and we hardly know them!

I've omitted such contemporaries as Thomas Merton only because writing by and about them is easily available. Finally, I selected these fourteen because they have helped me. I write from my experience and study over the years, and these mystics continue to nourish my heart and inspire my journey. I pray that they may do the same for you.

In those I've selected, as well as many others, the Christian spiritual tradition came vividly alive. They knew what it meant to love God, to want God, to actively seek his love and cooperate with his grace in their lives and hearts. In the end, they experienced God's infinite beauty in their own lives. The mystics are our Christian treasure.

Because we have long neglected them, we may not know how immensely valuable to us their lives and experiences are. They can be daily companions, bringing inspiration and instruction. They interpreted their experience within the culture and the Christian theology they knew. They pondered the meaning of their experience for human life and even for the universe. They usually did not emphasize their own experiences, except when telling them seemed to further the purpose of God to reach others. They leave many of our questions unanswered, but they give us enough to begin with new interest and determination to find the God our heart so urgently desires.

Although the mystics are not always easy to read, help comes through their writings. After all, we do believe in the communion of saints, do we not? If we can pray to saints to find lost objects, surely we can read the works of a great mystical saint and then pray to her or to him for guidance and support. We share the same longing, the same goal, the same Christ. We all belong to one Body. The mystics are there for us, praying for us every step of our way to God.

When we examine the lives and writings of the mystics, we may not agree with everything they thought. One of the clearest differences we often find is their heavy emphasis on ascetic practices that seem extreme today. Mystical writings are not divine writ. They have come from the experience of human beings, experience that is partially linked to time and place. We are free to use what we can and skip the rest. Furthermore, each was an individual. God tailors the path to individual needs and capacity. So the mystics are never to be dictators for us but excellent guides and companions on the way.

Whatever help from them we choose, we need to remember always what Meister Eckhart wrote: "When people find themselves unequal [to the saints], they think that they are far away from God....No one ought ever under any circumstances to think himself far away from God, not because of his sins or weakness or anything else...wherever a person may go, far or near, God never goes far off. He is always close at hand."[4]

Of course, all Christians—mystics or not—have much in common with one another. We enjoy the same faith and basic doctrines, though particular interpretations legitimately vary. Standing in this shared faith, we can look at individual and cultural differences as needed so as to gather a whole pattern of understanding and practice for ourselves.

WHAT IS SPIRITUALITY?

Before we explore how we ourselves can adventure in spiritual growth, let's ponder that word *spirituality*. It has been much misused recently in our all-pervasive media, and some are inclined to think it is an invention of "New Age" adherents. It is not. Spirituality in general is the innermost aspect of religion. Christian spirituality is the inward journey of the human spirit into the very heart of God, to dwell there with Christ and the Holy Spirit in full awareness forever.

A few notions about spirituality need immediate correction.

♦ *Spirituality is not "pie in the sky by and by."* As we have seen, the kingdom of God is for now in this very life.

♦ *Spirituality is not merely being a decent citizen or even a reformer.* Of course, we may choose to express our own spiritual life in the world through social action.

♦ *Spirituality is not simply a moral life.* Of course, spiritual development is not possible without basic morality.

♦ *Spirituality is not psychology.* However, we may become healthier psychologically in the course of our journey.

♦ *Spirituality is not something separate from the rest of life.* This is the most insidious misconception of all. In truth, spirituality eventually will pervade every moment of life—even when we balance the checkbook, make love, or drive in traffic. Everything we do and everything we experience will be enhanced by our own spiritual development.

We have seen that a spiritual life does not require a different "state" in life. In fact, some conditions of family life or work life are actually more advantageous to a deep life with God than life in a monastery is. We can begin precisely where we are. In fact, that is the only place we can begin.

Since spiritual life is an inward journey, no particular externals are required. When we turn within deeply and consistently enough, we will find God in our heart and ourselves in the loving heart of God. This is simple enough to say, simple perhaps even to understand with the mind. To live it is a great challenge, a fabulous adventure, a fascinating journey. Ultimately, it is coming home to our true home, the "place" we have yearned for always: the heart of our Creator.

Even though our heart longs for God, it seems almost audacious to think that God wants us just as much, or even more, than we yearn for him. God is the initiator, always, of our longing. But more, Bernard tells us that

God is the cause of loving God....He himself creates the longing. He himself fulfills the desire. He himself causes himself to be such that he should be loved. He hopes to be so happily loved that no one will love him in vain. His love both prepares and rewards ours. Kindly, he leads the way. He repays us justly. He is our sweet hope. He is riches to

all who call upon him. There is nothing better than himself....He gives himself.[5]

That has been a great wonder for all lovers of God. They have
consistently asserted its truth. Because of God's compassion—of
what God *is* (see 1 John 4:8)—he comes to us. He comes to us faster
than we ever wish to come to him. It is said that for every single step
we take toward God, he takes a dozen toward us. It's a fact that never
stops astounding us.

GOD'S IMAGE IN US: CREATED FOR HOPE

Two pilgrims bumped into each other on the road to the Holy City.
They collided because the man was blind and the woman was lame.
As they commiserated together, they realized that neither would make
it to the Holy City alone. The blind man kept wandering off the road
and running into things. The lame woman stumbled and fell too often.
So they decided to collaborate. The blind man, who was strong, would
carry on his shoulders the lame woman, who could see the road. Then
the seeing woman could guide the journey, and the walking man could
carry them both. Together they would arrive in the Holy City of their
hearts' desire.

The blind, but strong, man in this tale is method, the "how to" of
spiritual life. The seeing, but lame, woman is wisdom, who sees the
overall journey and intuits the next steps. (Of course, it is not important which is male and which is female—in tradition, wisdom is
feminine.)

So we need an overview offering us some wisdom and perspective
and information about how to go forward. Theology belongs to the
wisdom part of the path. All of us have some notion of Christian
theology. Here, let's consider two theological notions that will provide a framework for our "how to" information.

Our first basis for spiritual hope is found in Genesis 1:26-27: "Then
God said: 'Let us make man in our image, after our likeness....' God

created man in his image, in the divine image he created him; male and female he created them." Genesis 2:7 adds that our life is the breath of God. What does it mean that we are created in God's image, that we are like him and have his breath in us as life itself?

It means that God's intention for us is totally good, for he has made us like himself. Within us are goodness, intelligence, excellence, skill, freedom, love, and tranquillity. In the deepest part of our inner being, God dwells, for we are like him there. This is the very nature of our creation. Meister Eckhart put it this way: "Know, then, that God is present at all times in good people and that there is a Something in the soul in which God dwells. There is also a Something by which the soul lives in God...."[6]

But we often neither experience nor express this Something or these divine qualities. Why? Christian understanding says it is because of sin, which entered quite early into human existence. Sin has been variously defined. Gregory of Nyssa understood it to be the deprivation of goodness. That is, sin has no definite existence in its own right. It is what humans do because they lack awareness of their own profound goodness. So we act in disobedience to God. Since this seems to have been the case almost from the beginning, it is called "original sin."

Some Christians have thought "original sin" meant "original guilt." That is not the best insight into the teaching, however. Rather, "original sin" is an "original wound" in our nature caused by disobedience. It is in our human nature that something has become deeply injured. It is this into which we are born—not into individual guilt that we must shoulder. So the question "Why should I be held accountable for something Adam and Eve did?" is meaningless. We are not held accountable for it.

If we do not like living in a wounded condition, healing is available in God. The spiritual life may be thought of as a healing journey, for that is indeed what will happen along the way. We will be healed until we are whole—and wholly like Christ.

Until then, however, we are affected by original sin. The reason is that human *nature*, as early Christian mystics understood, is one single thing. It is not a collection of separate individualities, as if each of us were totally divided from all the rest. We share a common human nature. Our nature, according to early Christians, was and is affected by the human refusal of goodness.

We can understand this, can't we? After all, if my grandfather was an angry person, then my father was affected. Whatever my parents were affects me and my children as well. It is as if our earliest ancestor ignored his created goodness and passed on his deprivation of goodness to all the rest of us.

According to Christian understanding, God saw perfectly well the injustice of keeping all humans forever shut away from his goodness. So he took upon himself our shared nature and made it divine in Jesus Christ, who then was the full and complete eternal Image of God, the divine Word deep in every human being. The Incarnation thus restored human *nature* to its original created capacities—the qualities of God. Because of Jesus, the individual human being is invited to actualize that Image in his or her own individual life.

Gregory of Nyssa viewed the Image of God in humankind as our most essential nature, distinctively human. "The heavens were not made in God's image," he said, "nor was the sun, nor the stars. You alone are a copy of the Being who is above all thought, a similitude of the incorruptible Beauty, and a reflection of the true Light."[7] In that image is our human glory and our greatest hope.

That glory is severely tarnished, however, we must admit. In fact, it is so covered over with the mud of godless living that we may have lost sight of it altogether. Early Christians thought of the Image as a mirror, capable of perfectly reflecting God within our own being but now covered over with junk—junk we all recognize and feel and struggle with inside ourselves as well as outwardly.

Yet the Image of God has not disappeared; it lies hidden, as it were, within us. Through Christ, we are enabled, if we wish, to clear away the trash and polish the mirror once again, so as to experience the truest inner reality as Catherine of Siena did. She wrote:

By the light of understanding within your light, I have
tasted and seen your depth, eternal Trinity, and the beauty
of your creation. Then, when I considered myself in you, I
saw that I am your image. You have gifted me with power
from yourself, eternal Father, and my understanding with
your wisdom, and...a will, so I am able to love....[8]

Her experience is matched by mystics across the centuries. Gregory
of Nyssa, in the fourth century, says, "If you but return to the grace
of the Image...you will have all you seek in yourselves...God is
indeed in you."[9]

Bonaventure, in the thirteenth century, says that if we enter within
ourselves, "the light of truth glows upon the face of our mind, in which
the image of the most blessed Trinity shines in splendor."[10]

The fourteenth-century author of *The Cloud of Unknowing* (cited
hereafter simply as *Cloud*) says, "He fits himself exactly to our souls
by adapting his Godhead to them; and our souls are fitted exactly to
him by the worthiness of our creation after his image and likeness.
He...is fully sufficient, and much more so, to fulfil the will and the
desires of our souls."[11]

What a magnificent hope! Because the Image of God is already
there, in the innermost spaces of our very own being, we may find
God, know him, experience him, love him. He waits for us there.
The possibility of living fully in him is built into our being. We
don't have to move the universe. We have only to throw out the trash
hiding God's image and learn to meet him within our own depths. To
believe that, even a little, is enough to inspire us to get on with the
pilgrimage.

So the Image of God in each of us humans is a given. We can count
on it as we journey inward, homeward to God. Bonaventure points
the way: "We must pass through [what is] material, temporal, outside
us. This means to be led in the path of God. We must also enter into
our soul, which is God's image, everlasting, spiritual and within us.
This means to enter in the truth of God. We must go beyond to what
is eternal."[12]

DEIFICATION: THE GOAL OF OUR CREATION

If the Image of God in us is the beginning of our hope, how can we think about our goal? Is there a wise idea of what we are undertaking? Yes. For the first seven hundred years in the Church, the spiritual life was called "theosis," which in Greek means simply "deification," that is, being made into God. In many of the early writings, "Christian life" means precisely the process of deification. By no means was it exceptional. Jesus Christ, God Incarnate, was held so dear because he made deification possible for otherwise ordinary humans.

This particular teaching has been almost completely forgotten in the western Church. Its truth has never been challenged. It has merely been ignored. In the Orthodox churches, it is better remembered and forms a powerful basis for understanding spiritual growth. So before we discover the "how tos" of our spiritual journey, let's think about deification, to better understand our goal.

In the earliest Christian writings we have, the mystics speak very boldly of this astounding possibility of Christian deification. They say it plainly: God became human so that humans might become God. Or, put another way, he became what we are so that we might become what he is. Or Jesus Christ was God by nature; we may become God by grace. Meister Eckhart, too, says it plainly: "The first fruit of the Incarnation of Christ, God's Son, is that man may become by the grace of adoption what the Son is by nature."[13]

This does not mean that you or I, as individuals, become the creator of the universe and master of all. That is the idea of the prideful ego-self. The distinction is vitally important. Deification means that our being can be totally transformed into God's own nature and that we may experience that transformation. Then we will actually participate in God, as stated in the Second Letter of Peter: "He has bestowed on us the precious and very great promises, so that through them you may come to share in the divine nature..." (1:4).

Maximus the Confessor returns to this subject again and again. Here is one of his descriptions:

When Christ who has overcome the world has become our leader....He sets in movement in us an insatiable desire for himself....When we fulfill the Father's will he renders us similar to the angels...as we imitate them by reflecting the heavenly blessedness in the conduct of our life. From there he leads us finally in the supreme ascent in divine realities to the Father of lights wherein he makes us sharers in the divine nature...and [we] become clothed entirely with the complete person who is the author of this grace, without limiting or defiling him who is Son of God by nature.[14]

We may never have been aware of this idea, yet it is available to us in the Mass. At the beginning of the eucharistic part of the liturgy, when the priest mixes the water with the wine, he prays (inaudibly or aloud): "By the mystery of this water and wine, may we come to share in the divinity of Christ, who humbled himself to share in our humanity." The Christian community actually prays for deification in every Mass, though few of us pay attention to it.

The strongest statements about deification, however, are found in John's Gospel. Jesus says, "You will see me, because I live and you will live. On that day you will realize that I am in my Father and you are in me and I in you" (14:19-20). And again, he prays that all disciples may be one "as you, Father, are in me and I in you, that they also may be in us...so that they may be one, as we are one, I in them and you in me, that they may be brought to perfection..." (17:21-23).

It is mysterious, this oneness that includes God, Christ, and potentially ourselves. But this much is clear: Jesus wanted for us his own experience, that we be one with and in God as he was. And God himself wants it for us, because not only did he make us in his own image, so that being essentially like him we could be one with him, but he took human nature on himself in Christ to make it possible for us.

As God invites, so he sustains us and guides us along our way. Then in the end, when we are strengthened and purified, when we have become much like God and totally receptive to him, God gives the goal: transforming union with him, fullness of deification, all of himself.

Surely, since God wants us to become one with him, we can rely on him to give us whatever we need for the long journey home to him. God in Christ is, as Jesus said, the way itself (see John 14:6a). He will never abandon us to travel alone. We can depend on God to show us what we need for the next step.

God does not force us to himself, however. He always leaves us totally free to say yes or no to this most stupendous of invitations. Moreover, we are able to stop at any point along the journey (though that does seem incomprehensible). God lovingly invites us to become, by the constant help of his grace, what he is.

It is not automatic that we will want or undertake the inward effort to become what Christ was in the Father. Since we are invited, we must give a definite yes to the process. We must choose it. Our yes will be rooted in our longing, our restlessness, our love of beauty and joy, and in love itself. Our yes implies that we are willing to do our part to cooperate with God's grace in this amazing and awesome undertaking. If we accept the invitation, we pledge ourselves to go inward with determination and with as much effort as it takes.

As Maximus says, "Thus if any one wishes to have a life and condition that is pleasing and acceptable to God let him do what is best and noblest of all. And let him as best he can take care of the soul which is immortal, divine, and in process of deification."[15]

That we must choose the journey and act accordingly is one meaning of Jesus' parable about the wedding banquet in Matthew 22:1-13.

Some who were invited did not say yes; others did say yes and joined the festivities. Even then, the one who came improperly dressed was thrown out: "Then the king said to his attendants, 'Bind his hands and feet, and cast him into the darkness outside, where there will be wailing and grinding of teeth' " (22:13). So we must do our part.

If we choose to say no, God's invitation holds, and life goes on however it does. If we say yes, even a mixed and uncertain yes, life is changed forever. It begins to open into the most astounding and glorious adventure available to human beings. It will last a lifetime—and more, into infinity.

If we say a conscious, considered yes to God's gracious urging in our heart, nothing in our life will be the same as it would have been without our yes. From that moment, the Holy Spirit takes a far more active role in every circumstance of our living. The unexpected becomes the norm for us, as God draws us nearer and nearer.

Even then, all God's action in us remains exquisitely sensitive. Never is our freedom violated in the slightest. Neither are we ever abandoned (regardless of what our emotions may try to tell us).

Gregory of Nyssa offers two important ideas that clarify how our journey works. At its beginning, he says, we exercise the truest free choice any human can have: the choice to begin the return to God or not to begin. In his time this was an adult choice, and a yes answer resulted in baptism. Today, since many of us are baptized as infants, we have no adult ceremony to mark this momentous interior yes. But God hears it in our heart no less clearly, and he responds immediately. After all, it was his idea! He has been encouraging us inwardly—although perhaps secretly—all along.

Anyway, Gregory says we experience God's invitation as a certain emptiness inside or as a deep desire within, and we say yes. Then God fills the space we have experienced with something of himself, at the same time enlarging it, so we feel a sweet longing for more of God. That longing helps sustain our efforts on the journey. Then, says Gregory, when we have enough "new space," God gives us more of himself. Simultaneously, he enlarges our capacity again. And so it goes: ever more longing for God but never frustration; ever more receiving of God but never satiation.

"The soul that looks up towards God, and conceives that good desire for His eternal beauty, constantly experiences an ever new yearning for that which lies ahead....Hence she never ceases to stretch herself forward to those things that are before, ever passing from her present stage to enter more deeply into the interior...[and] each newly won grace always seems to be more beautiful than those she has previously enjoyed."[16]

It is like an ongoing spiral into God's very heart. We may not always be able to identify every movement, and the spiral may sometimes seem unclear to our rational mind. Gregory says it is reliable, however, because God is the one who does it, and God is totally faithful to our journey.

Then Gregory tells us that deification is an infinite progress. "…the graces that we receive at every point are indeed great, but the path that lies beyond our immediate grasp is infinite…those who share in the divine Goodness will always enjoy a greater and greater participation in grace throughout all eternity."[17] There is always more and more and more, forever moving more and more profoundly into the heart of God. Of course, from where we stand now, our mind gets lost trying to imagine this. It is truly beyond our thinking, kept sacred, as it were, for the deepest capacity in our souls.

Maximus taught that God will deify us, that is, draw us fully into himself and transform us in that union *inasmuch as we deify ourselves.* He assured his readers that humans have "the ability to deify themselves, through love for God's sake."[18] So we are not without potential! It is the everlasting paradox of grace being everything and our effort being necessary.

Clearly, deification is a gift of God. We cannot "do it" by ourselves. Yet we will not be transformed without our will and our determined cooperation. In order to be one with God, we must be like him. Only two who are alike can become one. So Maximus points to the necessity of our own intense efforts to become as much like Christ as we can when he says, "While we are in our present state we can actively accomplish the virtues by nature, since we have a natural capacity for accomplishing them. But, when raised to a higher level, we experience deification passively, receiving this experience as a free gift of grace."[19]

We must do all we can do, and God will do the rest. It is important that we fully see both sides. We must work at it, indeed, and very hard. But we work full of hope and certainty, because God will fulfill and complete our efforts. It is what he desires to do in us, even when we don't desire him. How much more we can count on him when we do desire life in his heart! There is absolutely no reason to think that deification cannot happen or that we are not worthy and so should leave it alone.

Of course we are not worthy—yet! We must cooperate with the Spirit to become worthy to the extent God grants it. When Maximus speaks of "deifying" ourselves, he means we must undertake to become as much like Christ as we can. What is beyond our genuine capacity will be given, and our capacity will be enlarged.

Seen from a deeper angle, we are indeed worthy. Our most real nature is the Image of God. Is not God worthy of God? We are the Image of God collectively as the whole human race, and as individuals, we are the Image of God potentially. Each of us may allow that image to become our primary identity in the world. That is surely worthy!

So it is our deepest nature, as Image of God, and our highest possibility, as Christians, to follow Jesus into full union with the Father. We, too, may "realize that I [Jesus] am in my Father and you are in me and I in you" (John 14:20). We may rejoice totally in God's invitation to be deified, to live totally in God's invitation to be deified, to live totally in him. If we wish, we may enter the journey full of joy and confidence as well as humility before the wonder of such a possibility.

ONLY ONE REASON FOR SAYING YES

There is only one good reason to undertake this spiritual adventure: the longing of our heart, which itself is our love for God. If we love God and want to live in him, we may journey inward. The "affection of love excels among the gifts of nature, especially when it returns to its source, which is God."[20]

Some will be tempted to say, "Well, if deification is what Jesus came for, I guess I should get going." Others may say "The Church insists that I go toward God; therefore, I should." This *should* feeling is not a good reason to do it.

If we feel no desire for it but only a sense of obligation, we will tangle ourselves in so much guilt that we will be paralyzed and go nowhere. It's better not to go at all than to try to force ourselves to it out of guilt. Our moral "shoulditis" can strangle us.

The truth is, the spiritual life, the inward journey into God, is not obligatory at all. Some things are obligatory in Christian life. They have to do with the moral commandments to be a decent, concerned citizen and not destroy other people's lives or the world we share. We are obliged not to be unduly selfish, and we are obliged to share our means with the poor. We are obliged to live upright lives in our Church and community. We are not *obliged* to become mystics, that is, to seek union with God.

It is true that in the beginning, no one's motives are pure. Birgitta of Sweden wrote of "two kinds of people. Some love God with all their heart. Others want to have God, but the world is sweeter to them than God is."[21] I suspect most of us belong to some degree in the second category. We may desire God, but we also would like some fine experiences and maybe a little recognition or power along the way. We might also hope that we would get some material rewards before we quit this body.

We need not worry. Our impurities will be healed along the path if we keep going. Bernard assures that "the more you grow in grace, the more you are enlarged in faith. Thus it is that you will love more ardently and press more confidently for that which you know you still lack. For 'to him who knocks it shall be opened.' "[22]

Spiritual growth, then, is pure invitation, pure gift. We may have it, if we want it. If we are not interested, the sky will not fall on our heads, God will never hate us. I personally feel that we will miss out on the most marvelous possibility of human life if we do not take this journey, but not everyone will agree with me or wish for it.

The question to each of us, then, is this: Do you, in some hidden corner of your heart, love God? Have you ever felt his touch in some secret or unexpected or beautiful or painful way? If you love God, and if you recognize God's invitation and want the gift of union that he is eager to give you, then—and only then—the spiritual journey to the heart of God is open to you. It is entirely up to you and me.

If we begin at all, we begin for love.

Notes

[1] *Writings From the Philokalia on the Preface of the Heart*, tr. E. Kad-loubovsky and G.E.H. Palmer (London: Faber and Faber, 1951), p. 120.

[2] *Meister Eckhart: The Essential Sermons, Commentaries, Treatises and Defense*, tr. Edmund Colledge, O.S.A., and Bernard McGinn (New York: Paulist, 1981), p. 167.

[3] *Bernard of Clairvaux*, tr. G.R. Evans (New York: Paulist, 1987), pp. 214-215.

[4] *Eckhart*, Colledge and McGinn, p. 266.

[5] *Bernard*, p. 191.

[6] *Meister Eckhart*, tr. Raymond B. Blakney (New York: Paulist, 1985), p. 133.

[7] *Light From Light: An Anthology of Christian Mysticism*, eds. Louis Dupre and James A. Wiseman, O.S.B. (New York: Paulist, 1988), p. 420.

[8] *Light*, p. 247.

[9] *Light*, p. 46.

[10] *Bonaventure*, tr. Ewert Cousins (New York: Paulist, 1978), p. 79.

[11] *Light*, p. 229.

[12] *Bonaventure*, p. 60.

[13] *Eckhart*, Colledge and McGinn, p. 162.

[14] *Maximus the Confessor*, tr. George C. Berthold (New York: Paulist, 1985), p. 118.

[15] *Maximus*, p. 197.

[16] Gregory of Nyssa, *The Life of Moses*, tr. Abraham Malherbe and Everett Ferguson (New York: Paulist, 1978), p. 268.

[17] Gregory, pp. 211-212.

[18] *Philokalia*, p. 278.

[19] *Philokalia*, p. 181.

[20] *Bernard*, p. 231.

[21] *Birgitta of Sweden*, ed. Marguerite Tjader Harris (New York: Paulist, 1990), p. 194.

[22] *Bernard*, p. 223.

General Principles
of Spiritual Life

A single essential movement underlies every step of the spiritual process. All of our efforts and all of God's grace contribute to this same movement. If we understand this movement—what it is and what it means—we have a touchstone by which to gauge every experience, every effort, every choice, every gift, that comes along as our interior life develops.

DETACHMENT

That central and essential movement is this: we become detached from all that is not God and we concentrate on God alone. When that change of orientation is complete, we experience God everywhere and all the time and everything we seem to leave left behind is returned to us in God.

Meister Eckhart praises detachment: "Detachment is the best of all, for it purifies the soul and cleanses the conscience and enkindles the heart and awakens the spirit and stimulates our longings and shows us where God is and separates us from created things and unites itself with God."[1]

What does *detachment* mean?

Eckhart describes it well.

> Perfect detachment has no looking up to, no abasement, not beneath any created thing or above it; it wishes to be neither beneath nor above, it wants to exist by itself, not giving joy or sorrow to anyone, not wanting equality or inequality with any created thing, not wishing for this or for that. All it wants is to be...detachment makes no claim upon anything.[2]

Detachment does not result in indifference to any part of life. On the contrary, it leads one to respond more lovingly and more effectively to all of living. Detachment is strong, a real attitude, not an absence of attitude. Maximus calls it "a peaceful state of the soul."[3] It is deeply interior and springs from a growing recognition of God's spirit deep within us.

Detachment from any particular thing means that we no longer relate our sense of identity to that thing, not in the slightest degree. We may observe, love, enjoy, even delight in what is before us, but in the heights of detachment, nothing will disturb the calm of our heart hidden in God.

Our inward response will tell us if we are detached from something. "Some owners have possessions without attachment, and thus do not grieve when they are deprived of them....But others possess with attachment and become filled with grief when about to be deprived."[4] So if we experience a feeling of regret when something is lost, it tells us that we are attached to that thing.

CONCENTRATION

Detachment is one side of the spiritual dynamic, the essential direction. The other side is concentration on God. Eckhart explains that "what you choose not to long for, you have wholly forsaken and renounced for the love of God."[5] Eventually, this concentration on God is total. Our actions, our choices, our fun, our enjoyments, our religious expression, our relationships, our work—all aspects of our living and ourselves come to be aimed in one single direction: love of God. That is the purity of heart that Jesus promised would bring results: "Blessed are the clean of heart, for they will see God" (Matthew 5:8).

Detachment and concentration are two aspects of one movement. Every little impulse toward detachment is at the same time a freedom to concentrate on God. And every thrust toward God, no matter how small, entails a little detachment from something else. "To be empty of all created things is to be full of God, and to be full of created things is to be empty of God."[6] Each is the flip side of the other. So every step toward one side has double worth, so to speak, because it is simultaneously a step toward the other side.

Concentration does not mean actively thinking only about God but rather never being unaware of God, since in time the focus of every experience is God. We eventually experience, with Angelus Silesius, the "wondrous mystery! Christ is the truth and Word, Light, life, food, drink, and path, the ending of my search."[7] We learn to live facing, as it were, totally in God's direction—and God's direction is inward. Indeed, outward experience will mediate God's presence to us. However, only deep within ourselves, in our innermost self, will we meet God directly, know God intimately.

Meister Eckhart describes concentration in the form of good advice: "A man should accept God in all things and accustom himself to having God present always in his disposition and his intention and his love. Take heed how you can have God as the object of your thoughts [when] you are in church....Preserve and carry with you that same disposition when you are in crowds and in uproar."[8]

Gradually, we learn to attend, with ever steadier awareness, to God within us at the root of our being. At the same time, we may be attending to the outward aspects of our life—doing the necessary, enjoying the beautiful, sharing in ordinary activities with others as usual—but within, we know a lightness and peace that hold.

We help ourselves by deliberate reflection, as Maximus suggests in his *Chapters on Love*, "Consider the things about [God], for example his eternity, immensity, infinity, his goodness, wisdom, and power which creates, governs, and judges creatures."[9]

In the beginning we will have to make an effort toward such reflection, for our awareness alternates between the external and the internal and more often focuses on the external. With time, grace, and effort, the balance will switch, however, and God in the interior of ourselves will become the stronger and determining aspect of our life. Then we can move ever more steadily homeward.

As we attend to God inwardly, we begin to want our daily choices to support this growing attention. We want our actions to be part of our total movement toward God. So we may practice at any time, taking our attention off our little concerns and focusing directly on God, offering each concern of the moment to God.

We help our decisions to support our inner movement by asking ourselves about each choice: *Does this bring me closer to constant awareness of God or does it not?* Some choices will be easy and clear. Some may seem tricky. But the very asking of this question will support the change in our orientation. That is what counts.

The shift toward concentration of our intention on God may seem easy in words, but it does require effort. Some have even called it battle; doing it, we become warriors of the spirit. It is hard because we are intensely attached to our ego-centric self—that in us which feels separate from everybody else, that claims much for its own credit, and that is full of desires for its own comfort. We identify ourselves with this "it" most of the time and call it "I." Yet as we go along, we know for sure that "it" is not all of what is in us. The true "I" is actually much larger.

Detachment from what is not God and concentration on God means that our ego-centric self, the smaller self that presently dominates our life, is gradually removed from its central position. God gradually comes to dwell in that position, from which all decisions are made, all impulses come, all fulfillments arise. Christ becomes the actual center of the Christian's life, vivid in one's experience. Instead of being self-centered, we aim to become God-centered.

This dynamic means living ever more consciously from the interior outward, rather than from the exterior inward. Actually, we always do live inside ourselves first, and what we are becomes mirrored in our external lives. But this is rarely conscious; furthermore, the interior we imagine we know is more often than not our ego-centered self. It is important to recognize that religion, as well as everything else in life, has its interior aspects and its exterior aspects. Many people never choose to activate the interior aspects of their Christianity, but the choice is always possible.

It is a fairly common recognition among the saints that the interior must occur first. "Do not misuse thoughts," Maximus says, "lest you necessarily misuse things as well. For unless anyone sins first in thought, he will never sin in deed."[10] Maximus puts it in terms of sin, but it is just as true of God or love or anything else.

As our life develops toward God, we come to know God within our heart. It is there that our attention increasingly rests. We come to value the growing interior life most because we can be close to God there. More and more, our decisions spring into exterior expression from this holy interior relationship. Our priority in life becomes our interior reality with God.

Although the struggle to change our orientation from our self-centeredness to God demands our total effort, its quality is essentially contemplative. As we go along, we will see more and more that it is rooted in silence, in quiet attention, in serenity and waiting and listening and loving. Above all, it cannot be hurried.

This change moves from the obvious that all can see to the hidden that only God and we ourselves know. The inner is hidden, not because it is deliberately held secret but because it occurs in the depths of our being, where some of the time even we ourselves cannot see it. Most of our spiritual growth takes place beyond even our own awareness. When it takes spontaneous expression, it may surprise us no less than it does others.

As inwardly we move away from transient things, we cease to live primarily for ourselves. We begin to live primarily for God. The mystics say over and over that they *want* to do, to be, only whatever is for the glory of God. Although this can sound pious to those of us who are more shallow, for the mystics it is burningly real: God and God's greatness made visible are everything they desire, all they cherish. They have come to see vividly how unimportant their own ego-wishes are in comparison to God's glory. "The perfect soul is the one whose affective drive is wholly directed to God," says Maximus.[11]

From this point of view, the lover of God knows that whatever he or she may offer to God, do for God, become for God, it is all only the work of a servant. It is for the servant to do what is asked. It is for the master to bring reward, if there is one. Certainly, the results of the servant's efforts are entirely up to the master. God is the gracious and loving determiner of all outcome. Ours is the offering, the living toward God.

This movement toward God is what Jesus meant when he said, "Seek first the kingdom of God." As we learn to do this, as we move ever more inward, we find that, indeed, all else is given just as Jesus said it would be: "So do not worry and say, 'What are we to eat?' or 'What are we to drink?' or 'What are we to wear?'…But seek first the kingdom [of God]…and all these things will be given you besides" (Matthew 6:31, 33). In every moment, every choice, put the priority on the inner life with God, and the externals of life will necessarily follow.

Here is a lovely comfort: If we miss something along the way, God will point it out to us, one way or another. We can trust that either God will show it to us for our action or God will take care of it directly. If our desire for God—the key to the whole movement—stays alive and increases, then whatever we miss will be shown to us at the right time.

In a sense, this movement is not as new as it feels to us. It is the return home—a home we may not recall consciously but one that is deep in our human nature. The reality cannot be traced fully, and it remains forever a mystery. But human nature was at home in God before creation. Human nature held God in Jesus. Our human nature cannot be at home with itself until we are fully aware of God at home in us. The spiritual life is the return to God at home in our own heart. That is our own true home. It is life eternal.

In "Little Gidding," T.S. Eliot wrote: "And the end of all our exploring will be to arrive where we started and know the place for the first time."

An instant's thought tells us that this transformation won't happen all at once. First of all, we're too scared to "detach" ourselves from very much in the beginning. The simple fact is that a sudden and total turnaround is actually *impossible.* If our initial experience of God radically intensifies our desire for God, we may *feel* transformed; but this must be worked out in daily experience. The change will be gradual.

We may find that comforting. Sudden change—even one so totally desirable as this—is not usually welcomed. We'd rather make changes gradually so we can adjust ourselves to them.

Changes will come, however. Every time we experience an inner shift away from something small toward something nearer to God, change in the externals of our lives will accompany that shift. Of itself, every newness will flow into expression in behavior and thought. Spiritual newness is powerful. It can be subtle and gentle or quite dramatic, but whichever it is, the power is real and will require adjustment on our part.

In the beginning, change will not be in outer behavior and action so much as an interior shift. We will keep right on living our lives in much the same way we always have, but our usual activities will not seem the same inside us. We will not be doing different things for a while, but we will be doing the same things differently.

As we experience a little of the fruit of detachment from all that is not God and increasing concentration on God, we may also find ourselves impatient for the process to move quickly. When we first experience, for example, a new freedom, we may wish for more of it—and soon! When we taste the love of God flowing consciously and unmistakably in our heart, we may wish it would just take over.

Since our reluctance in one moment can become impatience in the next, we may know that neither of these attitudes will help us much. If we can transmute them into deeper desire for God, they contribute to our journey. Always it is best to let God determine the timing of our growth because we seldom know ourselves well enough to be wise about it.

To this end, Meister Eckhart advises us again that one "is good when his intention is wholly directed to God. Set all your care on that, that God become great within you, and that all your zeal and effort in everything you do and in everything you renounce be directed toward God."[12] And our goal is like Saint Paul's, as Gregory of Nyssa describes him. We long to be able to say truly, "I have stripped away everything that is not Christ, and so have nothing in my soul that is not in Him."[13]

THE FOUNDATION IS GOD'S GRACE

No one can force an intimate relationship if the other party does not want it. In that respect, a relationship with God is similar to all others. We may want to be close to God, to share our lives intimately with God, and ultimately to be in union with God, but it will happen only when God gives it.

God gives, and wants to give, all of himself to us. That is God's own nature: love is what God *is*. God's love absolutely does not depend on us. Julian of Norwich prayed to understand God's purpose and meaning in the visions she experienced. This was the answer she received: "Love was his meaning. Who reveals it to you? Love. What did he reveal to you? Love. Why does he reveal it to you? For love. Remain in this, and you will know more of the same. But you will never know different, without end."[14]

The mystics have always said that all they experienced and all they received of God was pure grace, freely given, for no cause. The truth is, life itself is a grace from God, as we have not asked for it. It is God's nature to give. If God were to withdraw his grace from us for a single instant, we would simply not be—poof! There is nothing in our life that is not filled with God's grace (though often there are places in our life where we have not yet learned to see God). Our breath itself is God's. "The LORD God...blew into his nostrils the breath of life, and so man became a living being" (Genesis 2:7).

So God is instigator, initiator. From the beginning to the completion of the way, God is the active partner, grace the dominant force.

No matter how it may sometimes feel to us, we are the receivers of all the divine bounty, as Julian saw. "His goodness fills all his creatures and all his blessed works full, and endlessly overflows in them."[15]

We are but responders to the divine Word of invitation. If it sometimes seems as if the whole thing was our own idea, we have not yet looked deeply enough to see that in our very creation, our own nature, there is a "God-shaped" space, waiting, yearning to be filled with God. "Our soul is created to be God's dwelling place," as Julian reminds us.[16]

God stoops to our illusion of self-sufficiency and invites us out of it into full union with himself. "For we cannot be exalted to the Most High unless the Lord stoop to the humble and exalt the meek."[17] More than that, God gives us everything we need to make that journey and to bring it to completion—even though it is certainly God, and by no means we ourselves, who completes it.

For our life, then, and certainly for the spiritual life, grace is everything. Grace is the beginning and the middle and the goal. All is gracious gift. Nothing *can* happen without grace. There is no such thing as a spiritual do-it-yourself project. Bonaventure makes it plain: "No matter how much our interior progress is ordered, nothing will come of it unless accompanied by divine aid. Divine aid is available to those who seek it from their hearts."[18]

The more we ponder this truth of grace, the more we will let go of trying to control the whole course of our journey. In the beginning, it is easy to imagine that we are the dominant partner, the one who decides and acts and makes things happen. However, that is only because we do not yet see well; we are still in illusion about what is really happening. We will help ourselves if we let go of that notion as quickly as we can.

Julian heard God saying, "See, I am God. See, I am in all things. See, I do all things. See, I never remove my hands from my works, nor ever shall without end. See, I guide all things to the end that I ordain them for, before time began, with the same power and wisdom and love with which I made them."[19]

Precisely because the whole enterprise is grounded in God's grace and is gift, we cannot control the outcome. God will give himself when, as, and if God knows we are ready. And only God can know that. "For the great love which he has for us he reveals to us everything which is at the time to his glory and our profit."[20] So our best cooperation is to turn over the control and the results to God as soon as we are able. It may not be quickly and, at first, it will be piecemeal. Time and practice, however, will teach us to release even our own efforts into God's heart and leave them there.

God is everything on this journey.

COOPERATION WITH GRACE: PRACTICE, PRACTICE, PRACTICE!

Even though God is the beginning, the way, and the goal of our spiritual life, it is also true that the process requires our cooperation. "Indeed, the varied distribution of God's spiritual gifts is always in proportion to the efforts of those who seriously labor," says Gregory.[21]

God has created us to be free to respond to divine Love with a yes or a no—or a default, which is no. God has loved us into being and will sustain our life. God calls us to his love. God *never* will force us to anything. God loves, God invites, and God waits. The invitation is never withdrawn. So, as the old tennis cliché goes, the ball is in our court.

This book assumes our yes to God's invitation. Everything suggested here is based on it. Only if we have accepted God's invitation will we be interested in cooperating with God's grace in us. And our cooperation is the only part of the process we can actively affect. Everything else is God's own. So at the beginning of nearly every paragraph, the reader could recall that "this is said, *because* I have said yes to God."

If that is forgotten, the suggestions in this book could contribute to a whole mountain range of guilt. No one wants that.

Beyond Obligation

The crucial point is attitude. If all the practical actions we can take to cooperate with grace are thought to be in the slightest degree morally obligatory, we will be bound tighter than we have ever been.

For the one who has said yes to longing for God, ordinary morality and obligation are only a beginning. Moral living is *assumed* in the spiritual life. Cooperation begins beyond obligation. Cooperation is practice that is freely undertaken for the sake of divine Love.

Practices are "things to do" that we choose as cooperative efforts. Practices overlap and multiply one another's effectiveness synergistically. We can begin with any practice we wish but will usually choose one we feel drawn to and enjoy. We expect some modest fruit for our efforts in such a practice, and God may coddle us with obvious results in the beginning, though often not in the expected form.

A good attitude is: "This is practice." A practice, if it does not go well, can still be offered to God in willing cooperation. We can learn from it and continue forward without punishing ourselves with guilt. After all, since this is an invitation, we remain free. As the ads say, "You can cancel your subscription at any time." God will keep loving us—and keep waiting!

Just as with the choice to be an artist in any field, we choose our goal, then we do whatever we can to attain it. Sometimes we like what we do along the way, and sometimes we don't. But if we want to get there, we keep going. We practice—whether we feel like it in the moment or not. So it is with spiritual practices. Practices help us. They cooperate with God's action in us.

There is an important difference between spiritual and artistic practice, however. Spiritual practice can be done any time, any place, under any circumstances.

Inner attentiveness to God is instantly available. It requires no time (except for a period of daily quiet), but neither does it waste time on matters that are not beneficial. Whether we are sick or well, rich or poor, struggling or at rest, we can turn to God within our own being. The uneducated, those who don't enjoy reading, the economically disadvantaged—as well as their opposite counterparts—can turn within to God. This inner attention and all that supports it can be taken up by everyone.

All our spiritual practice, no matter how small or how challenging, will either help detach us from the transient or help concentrate us on God. Further, the effectiveness of every practice will be measured by how powerfully it accomplishes one or the other.

Certainly in this book, only a few of the almost countless possible practices are offered. Which ones we choose to undertake is not so important, as Meister Eckhart tells us, for "what one such practice could give you, you could also obtain from another, if they are both good and praiseworthy and have only God as their intention; everyone cannot follow one single way. It is the same with imitating the...saints. You may well admire and be pleased by practices you still are not required to imitate."[22]

Spiritual life is, then, essentially a simple matter to grasp. No one has yet found it easy to do because the layers of dirt over the Image of God in us are many and deep. But God is powerful enough to lift them all away if we want him to and if we cooperate. We can look forward to it with Gregory: "Once this...covering is removed, the soul's beauty will once again shine forth."[23]

TO BEGIN: WHERE ARE WE NOW?

When we want to take a trip, we need to know not only where we want to go but also where we are starting. We have some idea of our goal in spiritual life and we know for sure we are not there yet. Where are we now?

We begin the journey well, however, if we first recall that our essential nature is the divine Image within. Then we do well to acknowledge our messy and difficult current situation. That is not so hard. We know that life is difficult, with many struggles and pains, and that we feel more or less separated from God and everybody, encased in a skin with firm and sometimes unwelcome limits. We are presented, because of our wounded nature, with monumental challenges. We will take up these challenges one at a time and they will be overcome in us. There is no other way through this maze of original woundedness than to walk through it. Yet we move toward the most glorious goal in all of human experience: God fully alive in us.

Self-Knowledge Is Vital

If we were starting to build a cathedral, we would need a picture of the finished building. We would need an inventory of the materials we have at hand and the sort of ground we have to support the foundation. For a trip, we need to know both destination and starting point. So knowledge of ourselves is absolutely necessary and will remain necessary until the goal is fulfilled in us.

Our starting point is ourselves, exactly as we presently are. Self-knowledge has two aspects, equally important. There is the common human condition—something gone awry—in which we all participate. Then there is our individual being with all its qualities, habits, tendencies, and character. As the journey progresses, we learn more and more about ourselves in both aspects.

Another way we may think of our wounded human nature is also found in Scripture. Here the key word is neither *fallen* nor *original sin* but *sleep*. We are sleepwalkers. We go about our daily life asleep to the true reality of life, asleep to love, asleep to God.

Saint Paul exhorts his readers to wake up. "It is the hour now for you to awake from sleep. For our salvation is nearer now..." (Romans 13:11). And again, "Awake, O sleeper, and arise from the dead, and Christ will give you light" (Ephesians 5:14).

We do not usually think of ourselves as being asleep, of course. We imagine ourselves to be awake and fully conscious. Yet as we begin to learn about ourselves as we live, we find that we are not conscious. We function "on automatic." Our actions go on, but we are not present, not attentive, not aware, even of ordinary daily matters.

How often have we gone into a room, only to realize that we don't know what we went there for? Haven't we all "come to" when driving, realizing we don't remember the last several miles at all? We misplace and lose things—I've lost my glasses when they were right on my face! How often do we eat without tasting our food, "listen" to a conversation without hearing it, walk from here to there without the slightest awareness of either our body or our surroundings?

These are small everyday examples, but they indicate to us the truth about ourselves: we are seldom fully present to ourselves or to our activities or to those around us. How, then, can we be present to God? If we walk around in a state of sleep like robots programmed to exist throughout the day, how can we hope to know God? We must wake up to know God.

We can think of woundedness and sleep as similar. Our lack of conscious awareness is sleep, but so is our sense of distance and separation from God. If we gradually come to know God, we gradually wake up to God and all of God's creation. We are encased in the cocoon of our ego-centric selves, where we sleep and where our hearts are veiled from God. Our efforts to awaken will themselves show us more of our sleep in the beginning, just as our efforts to become good will show us initially in precisely what ways we are not yet good.

So we can see that this, our common human condition, is where we are. This is the place we begin our journey.

The second aspect of self-knowledge is to see *how* we are individually, our personal selves. This self-knowledge includes the body, the emotions, the mind, and all the qualities and habits that make up our personality and our character. Moreover, self-knowledge implies an awareness of how we are at every moment. Such awareness demands a strong, centered, and consistent attentiveness. It is difficult for most of us to learn.

In general, people are not drawn to self-knowledge. We easily fall into the habit of avoiding or even fleeing any clear knowledge of ourselves. We are thus blinded to the reality of our own being. Most of us are probably afraid of what we will find. We may vaguely feel somehow "wrong" and would rather not know how "bad" we really are. Or we may fear that nothing is inside or that we will be shown to be boring or otherwise unpleasant. Whatever our fears, they add up to a distaste for knowing ourselves.

Another aspect of our resistance to self-knowledge is our tendency toward self-deception. Whether we think we are better than we are or worse than we are, confusion about our actual state will skew the direction of our attention and also of our growth. If we think we are more or better than we actually are, we will miss opportunities to draw close to God in our weakness and to change that which needs to be changed. If we get stuck in being proud of our righteousness, then self-righteous is all we will become. On the other hand, if we think ourselves worse than we are, hating ourselves to some degree, we will be able to accept neither the love God offers us nor God's gracious help on our way.

Bernard takes the idea a step further. He says that "there are two things you should know; first, what you are; second, that you are not what you are by your own power."[24] One is trapped in unnecessary limitation when "he ignores the glory which is within him....And so we should greatly fear that ignorance which makes us think less of ourselves than we should. But no less...should we fear that ignorance which makes us think ourselves better than we are."[25] If we are unaware that the magnificent in ourselves is God's splendor, we lose the truth and the possibility of relationship to that truth.

So the spiritual life requires truthfulness about ourselves. If we are not yet truthful, it is not out of malice but from ignorance of reality. As we recognize that we do not know ourselves, that we value ourselves inaccurately—giving ourselves more credit for what is God's or not enough credit to our human nature as God's image—we can ask for God's merciful correction of our understanding.

No resistance is overcome in a day. If we want to know God, we must ignore our fears and go forward in increasing self-knowledge. Without self-knowledge, our goal in Christ is impossible. Julian of Norwich tells us, "For our soul is so deeply grounded in God and so endlessly treasured that we cannot come to knowledge of it until we first have knowledge of God....We must necessarily be in longing until the time when we are led so deeply into God that we verily and truly know our own soul; and as I saw certainly that our good Lord himself leads us into this high depth, in the same love with which he redeemed us, by mercy and grace...."[26] And on the other hand, "We can never come to the full knowledge of God until we first clearly know our own soul."[27]

So self-knowledge and knowledge of God go together because Creator and creature are forever bound together in the creature's very nature.

Spiritual progress comes from knowing ourselves profoundly—so deeply that we become aware that without God, we are nothing at all. This is the basis of true humility, of full recognition of all that we are in God's sustaining mercy and all that we are not in and of ourselves.

In her *Dialogue*, the Lord says to Catherine of Siena, "...you ask for the will to know and love me, supreme Truth. Here is the way, if you would come to perfect knowledge and enjoyment of me, eternal Life: Never leave the knowledge of yourself. Then, put down as you are in the valley of humility, you will know me in yourself, and from this knowledge you will draw all that you need."[28]

Here, then, is a major principle of spiritual growth: get to know yourself at every level. The very best place to do this is in everyday living. Life presents itself to the seeker of God as a mirror. It reflects back to us what we are like, offers us challenges and adventures, gives us help and comfort and the results of all our actions. Our self-knowledge is increased as we participate with awareness in all facets of life, whether in a family context or in single life, whatever our work and play may be.

A key practice in the pursuit of self-knowledge is self-observation. Evagrius, using the image of "demons" to refer to inferior inner habits, advises us that if anyone wishes to understand better one's own inner struggle, "let him keep careful watch over his thoughts. Let him observe their intensity, their periods of decline, and follow them as they rise and fall. Let him note well the complexity of his thoughts, their periodicity, the demons which cause them, with the order of their succession and the nature of their associations. Then let him ask from Christ the explanations of these data he has observed."[29]

Observation does not mean evaluation. Our approval of what we see is less important than seeing clearly whatever is present within, watching it, observing it, listening to it, attending to it. By practicing this, we learn much about how we are in life. We also learn by experience that we ourselves are much *more* than the bundle of thoughts, traits, and habits because we are also observer, the "I," the experiencer.

Self-observation is also not the same as introspection in the usual sense of that word. It is not a rummaging around inside to uncover the causes of our present state. In self-observation, we want only to see, not to try to figure out how we came to be this way, much less whose fault it is. We need only to know *how* we are. (If we want that to change, that is for another time, another practice.)

With increasing self-awareness, our sense of smallness gives way to an awareness of the Lord deep within us, full of love and peacefulness. Gradually, we find ourselves more and more conscious of our rootedness in God. In this way, we grow into knowledge of the Lord while we come to knowledge of ourselves.

As Catherine of Siena hears God saying, "...one comes to knowledge of the truth through self-knowledge. But self-knowledge alone is not enough. It must be seasoned and joined with knowledge of me within you."[30] This is why the effort to know ourselves is so vital. If in knowing ourselves, we will also know the Lord in us, then we are attaining our deepest desire, aren't we?

We can practice this self-observation by being consciously present to what is going on in us as we go about our daily affairs. For example, as a writer, I do much of my work at home. Sometimes I find myself doing unnecessary things around the house that amount to piddling and dawdling and staring at the refrigerator shelves. When I become aware of this, I do not just stop it and drag myself back to the keyboard. I allow the behavior to continue and take a look to see what is motivating it. Am I fleeing? Am I lazy? Am I taking a needed break? What is the root of the behavior within me?

As often as not, I find that I have forgotten God again and am wandering around the house like a lost soul. Awareness is the nudge

I need to recall myself and turn again to the love of God within. Not that I always welcome this turning! The ego-centric me is not necessarily happy to return to the freedom of God's love, for it wants only its own self-centeredness. So in this moment, I must choose with my will once again.

In this moment of self-seeing and of being aware of God within, I experience the deep division in my own being. In this experience of "what is"—of truth—I again have an opportunity to decide where I want my life to go. Do I want the Lord at the center even *now,* in this moment? The choice may seem small, but it is not necessarily easy. It is an oft-repeated choice to detach myself from whatever is not God and concentrate my inner being on God. The attempt to know myself deeply in this present moment provides this chance again and again.

As God says to Catherine, "Knowing yourself and knowing me...is more perfectly gained in time of temptation, because then you know that you are nothing, since you have no power to relieve yourself of the sufferings...you would like to escape."[31]

The "temptation" here need not involve a large moral issue. It is the yen of the ego to center on itself in this moment instead of on God. That is what causes our suffering, after all. And in the end, God alone can displace our ego centeredness, so he himself dwells in the center.

A large step toward self-knowledge is accepting responsibility for our own self, our own life, as it is. We cannot face ourselves and know ourselves until we are willing to be responsible for ourselves. Without that, we will continue to run away from self-knowledge; we will continue to refuse to look at our human nature and our individuality. No one else is responsible for the way we ourselves are, and we must acknowledge that and shoulder it if we want to know God.

We can never know what we are not fully willing to see, to acknowledge, to claim, and to offer to God for changing if need be. This kind of responsibility need not make us feel trapped in guilt. It implies a full acceptance of the facts as they become apparent to us—acceptance without blaming anyone or anything outside our own selves.

This call to accept responsibility for ourselves is one meaning of

Jesus' declaration to his disciples: "Whoever wishes to come after me must deny himself, take up his cross, and follow me" (Matthew 16:24). Just as Jesus carried the cross of human sin, was crucified on it, and blamed no one but forgave all, so we, too, must carry our own sin until we die to it completely and forgive all that we have heretofore thought were responsible for who we have become.

Until we are ready to accept responsibility, we cannot see, for we are still sleeping. Until we can wake up and see, we cannot know ourselves. And without knowing ourselves, we cannot know God.

We cooperate with God's inner prompting when we admit to ourselves and to God that whatever we see is true. Our selfish self would like to take a quick look and hide it away again. Full admission of our reality, approved or not approved, is a great reliever. It takes the pressure off. That is one of the advantages of confession, sacramental or otherwise. Straightforward admission of how I really am allows me to see beyond myself once again to God within my being. Then the ego's grip is somewhat loosened because God is there, offering the power for change that I do not have of myself.

As Catherine says, "As the soul comes to know herself she also knows God better, for she sees how good he has been to her. In the gentle mirror of God she sees her own dignity: that through no merit of hers but by his creation she is the Image of God. And in the mirror of God's goodness she sees as well her own unworthiness, the work of her own sin...."[32]

Both views are necessary: a continuing awareness of our sin and separation from God, the individual ways in which we are asleep to God, and the knowledge of our profound dignity as God's creation and image. It is a lifelong effort that will take us ever deeper into ourselves and, in that same movement, deeper into God. Let's recognize right in the beginning that self-knowledge will not be accomplished once and forever until we are fully unified with the Lord.

People sometimes assume that self-knowledge and its companion humility mean that we become fully and painfully aware of all that is wrong in us. That is true, but it is only half of the truth. The other half is that we become equally aware of our talents and gifts and the beauties in our hearts and our lives—and we know them to be gifts of God. That vision is sometimes more humbling than the acknowledgment of our personal miseries.

It is when we know *all* aspects of ourselves that we become truly humble and find God within us. It remains a circular experience. As we must know ourselves to know God, so we must know God to truly know ourselves, as Julian has already reminded us.

As a human being, each of us is a single being, a unit. Therefore, all aspects of ourselves are included in self-knowledge, and all aspects of ourselves are to be included in spiritual life. Nothing in us is to be ignored, but all is to be gathered into our single aim: to love God and to know God, becoming one with God forever.

Everything we are includes body, mind, emotions, psyche, soul, spirit, and any other "parts" of ourselves we may define. They have been variously defined over time. But always, they overlap. They affect one another. They go to God together. Language seems to require us to speak of the different parts of ourselves as if they were separate.

OUR INTERIOR REALITY DETERMINES OUR EXTERIOR EXPERIENCE

One of the most important realizations of our spiritual journey is that there is an intimate relation between our inner stance and our external circumstances. The saints have insisted that our inner state even *determines* our total experience, our emotional and behavioral responses to life, and thereby our circumstances.

Many of us resist this idea. We imagine it means we are guilty of everything that goes wrong, and we plunge into self-blame, especially if we already have a habit of kicking ourselves. Or, since we are unable to trace all the connections with our reason, we may reject the idea as untrue.

The interior self creates the quality of our life. Let's see if we can understand how that is true. We turn to our own experience. Two visitors step to the edge of the Grand Canyon. One is awed by the shapes, the colors, the space, the intricacies of the ancient rocks. The other takes a quick look, remarks on the size of the hole in the ground, and heads to the gift shop. Have they seen the same canyon? Physically, yes, of course. But because they are different inside, their experience of the canyon is different.

You can check this in your own experience, your own memories. Get together with a sibling and recall the same events. You may find yourself saying, as my brother recently exclaimed, "Wow! Were we in the same room?"

A little observation will inform us that when we feel love in our own heart, other people seem more loving. When we feel cut off from other people, they seem more distant. We know already that we see our own faults most vividly in others. We know that our concepts influence our choices, which influence our circumstances. The most powerful concepts and feelings inside us are often those of which we are unaware—another good reason for acquiring self-knowledge.

What has all this to do with spiritual life? The inner life determines everything else. When the inner life becomes fully, consciously, and steadily anchored in the experience of the loving Lord, then we will know the Lord everywhere, in everyone, every circumstance, and every thing. Eckhart wrote, "Whoever really and truly has God, he has him everywhere, in the street and in company with everyone, just as much as in church or in solitary places."[33]

When we fully possess God inwardly, we will be totally transformed because the God with whom we have been unified deep within ourselves comes to meet us in all the externals of our living. Then we fully experience that God is All, as he in reality is. Then we fully know the truth that all is one and that one is God. In that experience, we are finally at home.

All our practices and disciplines and God's own grace aim to transform our inner life, where reality is, so that God may find total expression in our exterior life. We will experience externally only what is already alive interiorly. So the interior of ourselves is the field we cultivate and offer to God for divine action, divine changes.

We know that we have some control over our inner experiences, concepts, opinions, emotions, thoughts, and choices. Therefore, the principle that the inner determines the outer is a source of hope for better experience. Outer circumstances are often beyond our direct control, but our inner life is available for God's work in us. Then outer circumstances become simply the arena in which we express our inner life and through which our inner realities are mirrored back to us, although most people who take the spiritual journey affirm that outer circumstances change as well.

If we wait until circumstances seem fortunate for our journey to God within, we will never begin. In fact, the reverse is true. We begin the journey inward, and then circumstances become precisely right to further our progress.

This obviously implies that our attitudes, our motivations, are vital. Fortunately, attitudes and motivations are available to our awareness if we look. We can then alter them if we choose. Chapter Three is devoted to attitudinal practices.

PSYCHOLOGY AND SPIRITUALITY

Today, especially in western cultures, we seem to have a passion for self-help and self-improvement. We want to heal our emotions, our bodies, and all previous traumas; we want to become whole, to fulfill ourselves, to become self-actualized, to acquire healthy egos, to unify our sense of self, to leave behind dependence and codependence, and to cure our addictions. The list goes on and on.

There is nothing wrong with any of these purposes. The fault lies in thinking that they constitute "spirituality."

Engaging in these various forms of psychotherapy, self-administered or otherwise, is not the same as living the spiritual life. They address issues of individual growth, and their goal is the ability to live independent and reasonably happy lives in our society. They aim to make emotional and conceptual adjustments in us so our living can be "healthy," our self-image "high," and our ego "strong."

The goal of spiritual life is different; it is full, transforming union with God in love. The motive also is different. Psychology wants to make me better, while spirituality wants me to know and love God totally. Some psychological efforts can serve spirituality; some do not.

Spiritual life is not about effective life in society. It is about deification—the transformation of being into the Highest, that is, becoming Christ by grace and by incarnation. It is incorporating Christ into ourselves inwardly, then allowing Christ to flow out into our expression in the world. Spiritual life is less about making ourselves into good and effective human beings (a psychological aim) than it is about giving ourselves to God and letting God do with us as he wishes.

Spirituality is not concerned with particular *forms* of action, issues to deal with, problems to solve. "Female spirituality" or "male spirituality," "single spirituality" or "priestly spirituality"—phrases like these only muddy the waters. Usually, when closely examined, they clearly refer to psychological issues. Yes, men and women, married and celibate, working or independently wealthy—these states do involve different issues. These issues may sometimes suggest the *forms* our spiritual disciplines will take or the *forms* in which we express our spiritual life. That is, the specific practices, disciplines, and expressions of spiritual life will indeed vary with individuals and groups (men, women, and so forth), but the essence is always the same.

Divine love is divine love whether one is male, female, single, married, white, black, or whatever. God is God for all humans. The essentials of spiritual life have to do with being human, and the exterior forms that spirituality takes are as varied as individuals are varied.

If by *spirituality,* then, one means the *forms* of spiritual practice and expression, it makes sense to speak of a spirituality for different groups of different states in life. But if *spirituality* refers to spiritual life as such, then it is inaccurate to think that it is different for different people. Moreover, the deeper one's life with God goes, the more commonality is found with others whose inner life is also deep—even across religious boundaries.

The mix-up between psychology and spiritual life would not matter except that it may limit our understanding. Thus, the confusion can prevent us from going as deep into God as is actually possible. Since spirituality seeks union with the Creator of all and is about the transformation of the inner being of the individual, it is a profoundly interior process—much "farther" inward than the emotions and thought-patterns commonly dealt with by psychology.

Spirituality is a superior effort to psychology and, therefore, it can use psychological insights and sometimes even psychological methods to further its own purpose. But when people think that a practice, an insight, or a concept is spiritual when it is really only psychological, then they may be prevented from seeing the true goal of the invitation God extends to all: conscious and transforming union with our Creator and divine Lover.

It has been said that one must have a healthy ego before one can have a spiritual life with God, but this is not entirely true. God is *at work* in people who seek him, and part of God's work is the healing of all aspects of a person. That does not mean that God keeps himself totally hidden from the person whose ego-strength is poor. The spiritual life can and often does become the foundation for other healing—emotional, mental, and physical—to occur.

It may be more nearly true to say that a vital spiritual life overflows into healing the psyche. Healing is part of the inner transformation. When healing and strengthening are required for a person to experience more of God, do we imagine God does not know that or that God can do nothing about it? Indeed, God is the director of spiritual life, and God is trustworthy to do what is necessary in us.

Of course, God may direct a person to a therapist or to some other contact with psychological insights. That may be the best beginning for some people. But if we demand that we "fix" ourselves and only then turn to God—well, that's simply a false notion. We can (and are lovingly invited to) go toward God right now, regardless of where we are psychologically. God will meet us where we are, give as much of himself as we can receive, and begin to prepare us to receive more. If that preparation involves psychological shift or psychological help, we welcome it by all means. We remember, however, that in itself, psychological work is not spiritual life.

Because each of us is a whole, our psychological aspects will sooner or later be included in our transformation. Indeed, for a while it may be in our emotions and thoughts that we are most aware of the changes taking place at a deeper level of our being. That is one reason we may have initial difficulty making clean distinctions between psychological growth and spiritual transformation.

Some aspects of psychological life, like personal characteristics, may in fact not affect spiritual growth at all. Living toward God does not make a formless muddle of anyone. Personal idiosyncrasies and the aftereffects of individual experiences will remain. Catherine was not Evagrius was not Hildegard was not Eckhart. Eckhart was as blunt as Bonaventure was gentle, and both found God within. Birgitta mothered eight children; Julian had none. Both came to know Christ. Some of the mystics always had a temper. Some were zealous in their reforming efforts. Others remained quiet and kindly. All lived in God.

In traditional Christian discussions of spiritual progress, the "purgative" way is usually mentioned first. As we move inward toward God, we do undergo a purification, which is experienced usually as profound healing of old wounds. They may be traumas, sins, unfinished events, failures. Whatever they are, when God knows the time is right, these hindrances will be brought to our attention for the purpose of healing. We may have to work at the healing, or the obstacles may be lifted away by the Spirit when we offer them to God.

Of course, in the process, we become healthier psychologically. But that is almost incidental as we press inward toward the God we seek in love and desire.

THE ROLE OF THE BODY

Given that spiritual life is essentially interior and that the whole of ourselves is involved, what can be said about the role of our body, our emotions, our thoughts, our memories?

In our Christian tradition, probably the best known spiritual discipline is physical asceticism: denying oneself food or bodily pleasures or even engaging in pain-inflicting activities like flagellations and the wearing of hair shirts. Some writings about the body seem to treat it as if it were the main obstacle to knowing God or even insist that the body is the enemy. The body has not always enjoyed a good reputation in Christian spirituality.

Today we find this view to be extreme. So have some other voices in the tradition, long before ourselves. Even among the Desert Fathers and Mothers, who were surely heroically ascetic, the point was never to punish the body but to be sure that the inner life was not controlled by physical needs and desires. To that end, they sought to learn what were their true physical needs and to meet them but not give their bodies one whit more. So they slept and ate only as much as was necessary—far less than we do.

Abba Anthony said, "Some have afflicted their bodies by asceticism, but they lack discernment, and so they are far from God."[34]

Abba Hierax said, "...if you are hungry, eat, if you are thirsty, drink; only do not speak evil of anyone and you will be saved."[35]

The body is a vehicle for the soul, the spirit. It bears within itself the Image of God, the essence of the Creator's life in us. We need it to complete the tasks, interior and exterior, given us by God. Catholic tradition even indicates that only what is attained in this body remains for life to come. Bernard wrote, "The spiritual creature which we are has need of a body which is necessary to it, and without which it cannot reach that knowledge which is the only way to the knowledge the blessed have."[36] Therefore, we should be grateful to God for the body and treat it well as God's gift to us.

So it is important to keep the body as strong and healthy as we can. Spiritual growth eventually means a great deal of intensity in the spiritual forces, which also affect the body. If the body is weakened, our spirit may be affected in turn. We support spiritual life by treating our bodies well.

In our time and place, we are unlikely to deprive the body too much. We habitually do treat our bodies badly, however, by indulging their slightest whim. Catering to taste and fragrance, overstuffed stomachs, sexual indulgence for its own sake, lying around too much (watching TV or whatever), sleeping as long as we possibly can—these and habits like them treat the body very badly.

God speaks to Birgitta: "I enabled man to have bodily rest and quiet in order to strengthen the weakness of the flesh and to make the soul gain power and strength. But because the flesh is sometimes imprudently insolent, one must cheerfully tolerate tribulations....I gave foods and the necessities of the flesh for the body's moderate sustenance and so that it might more vigorously execute the virtues of the soul and not be weakened by excessive consumption."[37]

To honor the body as God's gift and the vehicle of God's life would mean giving some attention to finding just what our bodies do need and giving it to them consistently but no more. Such an asceticism would be challenging enough!

Abba Poemen said, "...I think it better that one should eat every day, but only a little so as not to be satisfied."[38] Here again, the point is to do the necessary for the body, but to keep an edge on it and not allow it to go slack from being full. The same principle is to be used in regard to all physical needs: fill what is needed and leave the rest alone. Be as fit as is reasonable and healthy.

By doing this with respect and gratitude for the body, we include it in our spiritual support system. It becomes our friend on the journey and we actually "spiritualize" it and make of it a servant of God for us, and our servant for God's sake.

The main principle about the body is that it must not dominate life. If one is dedicated to interior life, one gradually subordinates everything else to that aim, including the body's needs. This means that we freely choose what the body will do—that the body does not determine what we do.

Amma Syncletica, one of the Desert Mothers, summed it all up. She said, "There is an asceticism which is determined by the enemy....So how are we to distinguish between the divine and royal asceticism and the demonic tyranny? Clearly through its quality of balance...In truth lack of proportion always corrupts."[39] The best principles for any age.

Here is an example. When we practice contemplative prayer, we require that the body sit still for the time of our prayer. If the body is underexercised or overrested, it will be restless and squirmy. If it is overfed, it will go to sleep and take our awareness with it. If it is constantly overstimulated, it will refuse to sit still, or it will relax so totally without stimulation that it will, again, go to sleep. If we wish to practice uninterrupted, quiet prayer, we will seek the right balance for our body so it will support our efforts instead of struggling against them.

One profound change can occur in us when we learn to master our physical desires: we come to know that our bodies are not ourselves.

Most of us are intensely identified with our bodies, even to the extent that we have a lot of emotion about what happens to them after we die. We generally do not speak about our bodies as different from ourselves, because we imagine them to be the same. The way our bodies look, the way our bodies act, the way others view our bodies— all these are taken to be about *us*. This is a false perception and one that drops away when we discover that our *self* includes a body but is much more.

Furthermore, our larger self may use the body to express our devotion to God, our longing for God, our love for God. All ritual action and gesture is intended to give the body a way of praying: genuflecting, bowing our heads, sitting to listen, and standing to pray—these are traditional Christian ways in which the body is connected to the spiritual life. One of the purposes of ritual is to bring the body to its own participation in spiritual awareness. Of course, no ritual act helps much if we are not aware, if we perform it like robots.

THE ROLE OF EMOTIONS

Closely connected to our bodies are our emotions. They too are a natural aspect of ourselves, not to be despised. Part of every human being, emotions give us the drive and verve we need, tell us when we're in danger, and otherwise serve our life in this world. Emotions are not bad, even the negative ones. When the aim is God, however, our perspective on emotion will begin to shift.

As with the body, we tend to identify with our emotions, to think our emotions *are* ourselves. If there is anger in us, we say, "I am angry." If there is excitement in our emotions, we say, "I am excited." As if in that moment, that emotion is the whole of ourselves! It never is.

One of the illusions of psychology seems to be the assumption that "what I feel" is the same as "what I am." Therefore, much psychological work is done in the area of emotions. As such, it makes a major contribution to more tranquillity in emotional life. Tranquillity of emotion offers strong support to spiritual effort. If we find help in this area from psychology, it is good to take advantage of it. At the same time, we will want to remember that emotions are only a part of ourselves and, in spirituality, not the most important part.

With time and practice, we discover that emotions can be observed without being denied or repressed or expressed, that we can choose emotions to a large extent, sometimes directly, sometimes indirectly. Then we know that our emotions are not our essential self, just as our body is a part of us but not the whole. We are the one who observes and chooses.

As long as we identify our *self* with our emotions, emotional reaction will continue to dominate our living. We tend to let emotions make our decisions for us, whether we experience those emotions as wonderful and positive or as negative and unpleasant. We usually allow our emotions to dominate our view of ourselves and of others, indeed of most of life.

One of the changes that comes with spiritual growth is that emotion ceases to dominate us. Then we experience the truth that beyond emotion is peace, as Evagrius describes, when "the spirit begins to see its own light, when it remains in a state of tranquillity in the presence of the images it has during sleep and when it maintains its calm as it beholds the affairs of life."[40] Then we know for ourselves that emotions have their rightful place, but they are not the master of our house. "The passions continue to live; it is simply that they are controlled by the saints."[41]

Moreover, emotion rightly understood and used becomes a strong, marvelous servant of God in us. Our emotions are energy, springing up to assist the body in its life on earth. They are a manifestation of life itself in us. So long as we do not identify ourselves with our emotions, they will serve every purpose we sincerely undertake. When we identify with them, they take on a life of their own and dominate our decisions. On our inward journey, we want to become like Abba Joseph, who once happily said, "I am a king today, for I reign over the passions."[42]

In "Challenges and Obstacles" (page 131), we will discuss practices for dealing with our emotions.

Finally, we usually assume that our emotions tell us the truth. Yet a moment's reflection will show us that it is not so. Our emotions fluctuate like the weather, only faster. Look at what happens in a single day. We grouchily get out of bed, then feel much better if someone is sweet to us. Our emotions swing downward in traffic and up again when something goes well at work, then down again when— well, you get the idea. We all know it, yet we miss the implication that emotions are not ourselves but changeable reactions to circumstances. Since emotions are less than our real selves, we can change them. It's a matter of practice.

If we want to seek peace, the peace that is God's, we do well to begin to disengage our sense of identity from our emotions.

THE ROLE OF THOUGHTS

Our thoughts and memories, then—surely they are our true and real selves?

Observation will quickly tell us that thoughts and memories are occurrences in the mind. They are not the Image of God we seek in ourselves. Like body and emotion, thoughts and memories are part of us, usually affect us, and are useful in their proper function. But, like body and emotions, they are not to be the dominant factor in our living. We can, with effort and attention, control our thoughts. Abba Sylvanus seems to have reached that high goal: "I have never let a thought that would bring the anger of God upon me enter my heart."[43]

In the West, we glorify the reasoning, extolling the mind as the guide to all good. Some of us may be more identified with our reasoning powers than with our emotions; if so, our thinking dominates our life. Certainly, we need the mind, and mental reflection can greatly support our spiritual effort. But since thoughts are less than God, just as body and emotion are less than God, that domination will sooner or later have to be changed. Then, like body and emotion, thinking will find its rightful place.

We want to remember always that God is beyond our thoughts no matter how brilliant or how correct, just as God is beyond our bodies and our emotions. When we seek God, we want to reach beyond these levels of ourselves and find God in our very depths. We leave them all behind in our efforts to know God. "Thought cannot comprehend God. And so, I prefer to abandon all I can know, choosing rather to love him....Say to your thoughts, 'you are powerless to grasp him. Be still.' "[44]

This is pointedly true when we settle ourselves to the practice of contemplative prayer. We can pray with our bodies, we can offer our emotions to God, we can pray with our thoughts—and do most commonly. Yet these are not the deepest forms of prayer nor do they bring us to meet God directly in our own being. For that, we practice contemplation, and then thoughts are clearly not our whole selves and, in fact, hinder our effort. "Leave them behind beneath a cloud of forgetting...and simply raise your heart to God with a gentle stirring of love."[45]

How can we begin to take steps to move these powerful parts of ourselves out of their central and domineering position? By regularly seeking silence before God. When we sit for silent prayer and try to face God directly and solely, everything begins to happen. The body may object. When it is stilled, emotions arise—hurt feelings from yesterday, pain from last year, confusions and angers, excitements and joys from a lifetime. If we merely observe them, just stay before them, as it were, and stare at them, they gradually subside. Or we may put them all in Christ's hands and allow him to direct our attention to himself. Likewise with all thoughts. When we simply watch, when we don't allow ourselves to be hooked by them and dragged away from our attention to God, thoughts gradually fade.

It is not a matter of getting rid of thoughts and memories but of giving them their proper place and making sure they do not dominate either our prayer or our life. "The reasonable use of thoughts and things is productive of moderation, love, and knowledge."[46]

It may take years to still the body, quiet the mind, and pacify the emotions. Along the way, we turn again and again to attend to the Lord within. We find ways of living that spring from our own center, that support our goal, and that do not arouse the inner noise of emotion and thought. Gradually, we learn to live for and from the Spirit, experiencing emotion and thought but free of their domination—free to be present to God in our heart's love.

As Evagrius says, "Happy is the spirit which, praying without distraction, goes on increasing its desire for God."[47]

DESIRES AND AVERSIONS

Thought, emotion, and body are closely tied to one another. What we do to help free ourselves from the domination of one will assist with the others. Our ego-centric self, our "self-ish" self, is found and expressed in all these facets of our everyday being. Our selfishness usually includes the desires of the body, the drive of the emotions, the concepts and opinions of the mind. These are *not* evil. They dominate us, though, and thereby usurp the position that belongs to God.

Taken together, these aspects of ourselves give us our attachments and aversions, our likes and dislikes, our desires and our repulsions. What we want and what we don't want affect everything we do and fill all our circumstances. They determine most of our decisions; together, they run our life.

The curious thing about desires or attachments is that they are never satisfied for long. Let's say we get something we want. We are pleased. Then, three weeks later (or much less!), we lose interest in what we previously wanted and we want something else. To this cycle there is no end, and a little reflection on our own lives will show it clearly to us. The same thing is true of aversions; we spend energy avoiding what we fear and dislike, insulating ourselves against the unpleasantness that can happen in life, protecting ourselves against whatever we find distasteful.

No wonder we get tired! Chasing after our desires and fleeing from our aversions takes a great deal of energy. We seem to squander it without considering that there is another way.

If we have a deep desire for God, however, the picture gradually changes. For our desire for God to be fulfilled, every other desire and every aversion will eventually be subordinated to that single, noble, and loving longing. Only by the desire for God above all else will the power be taken away from our habitual desires and dislikes.

Eckhart urges us onward: "Let us go on learning to abandon ourselves until we hold on to nothing that is our own. All our tempests and strife come only from self-will, whether we see this or whether we do not. We should put ourselves and all that we are in a pure cessation of will and desire, into God's good and dearest will."[48]

To follow Meister Eckhart's urging, we learn to base our decisions more and more on a new inquiry: will this choice serve my desire for God or not? Little by little we will be strengthened to choose only what leads to God in our heart, and to evaluate everything else by that standard alone. Then, truly, our emotional likes and dislikes, our body's demands and our reasons for doing what we've always done—all these lose their power to affect us. In this alone is there lasting peace.

Then we will know with Eckhart "the power in the soul that touches neither time nor flesh. It flows from the spirit and remains in the spirit and is wholly spiritual. In this power God is always verdant and blossoming in all the joy and the honor that he is in himself. That is a joy so heartfelt, a joy so incomprehensible and great that no one can tell it all."[49]

THE COMMUNITY OF LOVERS OF GOD

One principle of Christian spiritual life is that although it is intimately interior, it takes place in the mutual support of a community of like-intentioned people. Of course, there may be exceptions, but even Christian hermits have been in touch with other hermits.

Likewise, when family, the workplace—or both—are our everyday milieu, spiritual growth is enhanced by gathering regularly in community. This word *community* requires a little attention. Like so many other beautiful ideas, it has been trivialized in our time. Sometimes it is used to refer to an impersonal gathering of people who subscribe to common beliefs. Sometimes it means getting together for socializing—church suppers, bazaars, or bingo. Sometimes it means whoever comes to Mass on the weekend. We hear about "community building," which seems to mean that people should be in the same place and share an experience.

These are good things to do, but they may not offer much support for spiritual life. The notion of Christian community that I intend is that invisible but strongly felt bond that arises spontaneously among people who love God enough to seek him inwardly and to spend time in prayer every day and who desire that their whole self and whole life become oriented toward God.

If we know even one other person with this great intention, this hope, then we have a community. If we know several, we are fortunate. These, our real community, are a wonderful support. Gratitude flows out to God for the others who are also on the way and who live close enough to be able to share.

For spiritual life to grow maximally, the community can choose to nourish itself by encouraging its common life. This will imply regular gatherings. The frequency of meetings will vary with the desires and possibilities of the group. Some meet weekly for a short time, others meet every other month for a whole day away from home. Some plan to go to the same Mass, and the families sit together.

The most important part of such community gatherings is shared prayer. The form of their prayer varies with the preferences of the group. Sometimes it is silent contemplative prayer, sometimes verbal prayer of praise and intercession, sometimes the Liturgy of the Hours, sometimes petition. Many like to include a eucharistic celebration whenever possible.

There is usually time for personal sharing among the community as well. As we go along in our spiritual journey, everything imaginable comes up: unresolved issues, great joys, growth puzzlements, struggles, questions, wonderful insights, profound experiences of love. While these may be shared for the benefit of the experiencer, shared experiences often strengthen the community as a whole. Frequently, people find that their experiences fit precisely into another's need as they travel together toward God. The Spirit often orchestrates the experiences of community members as a means of deepening both their love for one another and their respect for each one's relationship with God.

It is in genuine community—people drawn together by their individual and common spiritual aim—that Christians will have their most beautiful experience of the Body of Christ. As we know, Jesus promised to be present whenever "two or three are gathered together in my name" (Matthew 18:20). Not only is the Lord's presence made nearly tangible in community gatherings but we experience him directly in one another and a lovely bond is formed among us. Here is the place of intensifying love for one another; that love, which goes beyond personalities and likes and dislikes, is God alive in our hearts.

When we seek intensely for life in God's love, we begin to examine all other aspects of our liking to see whether they support our inner intent. The company we keep will come under our scrutiny. This is a tricky area for most of us. On one hand, we prefer to be with people who support our aim; but on the other, we may feel obligated by our work or family commitments to be with some who do not support it.

Here are a few principles to aid discernment in this area:

In the beginning of our spiritual life, it is important that we protect ourselves. After all, we have little to give in the beginning, and the energy it takes for our own disciplines may be about all we have. More than one person has been harmed by exposing the new inner life to someone who is unsympathetic or scornful. Jesus warned us against this: "Do not...throw your pearls before swine, lest they trample them underfoot, and turn and tear you to pieces" (Matthew 7:6). In the beginning, discretion is helpful.

But aren't we supposed to take care of the needs of our sisters and brothers? Yes—but only as we are truly able to, and as an overflow of the love growing in our heart, not when it is motivated by an abstract notion of obligation. Many people have gotten intensely involved in "church-y" things and social action at the expense of their inner life, their families, their friends. That is questionable from the viewpoint of simple priorities. From the viewpoint of spiritual life, there is no question about it: their spiritual growth will suffer from too much action and too little silence with God.

While it is a common malady, it can be corrected if we ask whether or not our relationships support our inner life with God, then act accordingly.

We will also learn to recognize that some people's needs are beyond our personal capacity. They may be too emotionally needy for us, or they may be manipulative or merely seeking sympathy. Usually, we can tell when we have spent too much time with people like this because we feel inwardly spent and tired. It is not a good condition for prayer, at least until our prayer life becomes strong and steady.

When we reach out to people who are not "good company" to us in the supportive sense but whom we are moved by love to serve in some way, then we will be inwardly rejuvenated (though maybe physically tired) by our service. Then we will know that this service was willed by God and did, in fact, serve God in ourselves as well as in our sister or brother.

Keeping good company for ourselves includes seeking out contact with those who are ahead of us on the inner pathways, who seem closer to God than we feel ourselves to be. This may be personal contact whenever possible. If we know such people in our parish or our town, we may invite them to share food so we can also share a little of what is in their hearts—not greedily but as two pilgrims might talk about their travels.

We can also keep "good company" with the communion of saints;

it is real. The saints are available to us. They stand behind us like a great fortress, ready and eager to help and to protect us on our way. Some people may even see them during prayer, but many become aware of subtle "presences" around them, supporting, strengthening, comforting, even healing. And who knows when a helpful or healing or beneficial thought in our mind actually comes from an anonymous saint who loves our journey?

No matter how we experience the saints (and even if we never have), we do well to honor them, to be aware of their willingness to support our inner journey, and to seek their help. Reading about their lives makes individual saints more real to us. We might also "adopt" a saint, which was the original notion of patron saints. We may learn about and open ourselves to a particular saint with whom we feel an affinity. For example, because longing for God is such a vivid part of my own interior journey, I have "adopted" a saint whose life also included an intense longing, deeper than my own. I pray to her that my own hunger for God may increase.

What better company could there be than the company of the saints who have come to know and love God with the whole of their being and who now are in a position to support us with great love?

For Catholic Christians, one of the saints most loved and most often "adopted" in this way is Mary, the Mother of Jesus. She is revered as our mother as well as the Lord's mother. Many find it easier to lean on her maternal care than to connect with the Lord in any other way. While a relationship with Mary (who called herself the handmaid of the Lord) should never be a substitute for direct relationship with God, it is certain that she has been a great strength and help to millions of Christians across the centuries and continues to be today as well. There could hardly be *better* company!

SEEKING A SPIRITUAL GUIDE

The matter of a spiritual director is much discussed today. Most people embarking on inner life with God feel the need for a human guide, one whose experience and wisdom will support and advise them. Yet finding such a person—especially in one's own vicinity—is not always easy.

Spiritual directors in the Christian tradition go back as far as we can trace the forms of Christian spiritual life. Jesus was the first, as he taught and supported his disciples. His close followers became advisers and helpers in their turn, and so on. Among the early Desert Fathers and Mothers, there were the "old ones," men and women who were sought out for advice. As in any field, our spiritual life is greatly helped by the insights of another who knows it well.

Symeon the New Theologian wrote with the greatest reverence and gratitude about his own "spiritual father," Symeon the Studite. "He who gives himself in the hand of a good teacher will have no worries, but will live without anxiety and be saved in Christ Jesus our Lord."[50]

In earlier times, a seeker of God was advised to search for a guide who "can transmit into you the Light of Christ." These spiritual fathers and mothers bore their "directees" in their hearts, prayed for them by the hour, carried them like children in a spiritual womb. Such masters seem rare today. What, then, are we to do?

For many today, it is more practical to look for a spiritual companion or friend who also loves God and gives attention to the inner life but who may not be a "master." Often a friend who shares the same aim and who knows us well can offer insights that we miss, ask questions we haven't thought of, suggest resources we haven't yet found. Such a friend can also provide loving support for disciplines. Two people might even choose to be accountable to each other for their faithfulness to spiritual practices. With such a friend, the potential loneliness of the journey falls away.

A word of caution is in order here. Some schools today turn out "spiritual directors" as the result of fairly short academic, sometimes primarily psychological, study programs. While good spiritual direction may include psychological counseling, it must reach beyond it. Many graduates of these programs become wonderful spiritual directors with time and experience; others do not. People get into spiritual direction from all kinds of motives, not all of them helpful. The same applies to priests and religious. Some of them are wonderful directors; some are not called to it and should not be attempting it.

The caution is this: do not assume that academic training or religious vocation necessarily create a good spiritual companion. Choose your spiritual confidant with care and do not commit to a particular director/companion until you are sure he or she has the qualities you need and desire.

A good spiritual director will be further along the journey than you are, though this is not always easy to discover. She or he will have considerable personal experience in matters spiritual and will have read widely and received some training but—most importantly—will love God profoundly and firmly on the inner way to him.

It is probably best at the first meeting with a possible spiritual director to explore together to see if you are a good match for each other. Compare expectations, needs, experience, and understanding of this most delicate of relationships.

Any good director will understand that a spiritual relationship is God-given and must be good for both persons. She or he should not be ego-centric about this work and so should not be at all troubled if you decide not to continue the relationship if it is not valuable to you. Discern together and separately, pray about it together and separately, and only then decide whether this particular person would be a good spiritual companion for you. If you decide to continue, do so with the mutual understanding that the relationship could be ended at any time by either of you. Without the clarity of this freedom, the relationship can easily become skewed and detrimental.

It may be that you will be simply unable to find such a companion or even a community to share your journey. Someone has said if that is the case, you should throw yourself on the mercy of God and *read*. It is good advice. God will never abandon any of his children who seeks him in loving desire. A spiritual director, though an enormous help, is not absolutely necessary. Information about spiritual life, however, is. Much can be gained from reading about spirituality, especially in the writings of the mystical saints.

Good information is necessary because all along the spiritual journey, experiences vary, challenges come, previously unknown parts of ourselves surface, and decisions must be made. We need to know how others have experienced and handled these things, especially people who have received great gifts from God.

Then pray for a companion, a community, or both. In my experience, if we dedicate ourselves to the journey and do faithfully whatever we know should be done, praying all the while for human help as well as God's help, that prayer is answered. The form of the answer may be different than we expect, maybe even different than we prefer, but help will be given. It is ours to be open to God's help in whatever form it comes.

BE PRESENT NOW!

The principle that pervades all other general principles of spiritual life is that relationship with God takes place in the present moment or not at all.

That means, first of all, that the more we attend to what is going on right now, the more aware of God we will become. If we are aware right now—and right now—and right now—of God's presence, we will know God and find God in love in this very moment.

But how can I be aware of God in the midst of such a busy life, in the face of so many demands? The answer is by practice, practice, practice. There are many things we can do to help ourselves live in the present, where God is to be known, and some of these appear in the following pages.

Second, when a present moment has become past, we do well not to cling to it or try to revive it. This is often tempting especially in prayer. Something beautiful happens, and the next time we pray, we may wish to recapture it or re-create it. It simply does not work.

The same is true of the future. Trying to plan for experience of God in the future is as useless as trying to recapture the past. God is now, we know God now, we love God now, and we attend to God only in the now.

Ultimately, this is what eternal life actually means. "Eternal" and "everlasting" are not quite the same thing. "Everlasting" means going on through time without end. But eternal is timeless, it has no reference to time. We experience eternity in the present moment, the now. God is eternal, that is, God is beyond time, is timeless. God touches us in time, but Jesus wanted to give us "life eternal," that is, life with God beyond time.

The door to eternal life opens in the present, not in the future and not in the past.

So whatever our past life has been and whatever we imagine or hope or fear about the future, we are invited to allow it all and practice being aware of God within our heart in this moment, now. I suggest you stop reading right now and do just that....

Notes

[1] *Eckhart,* Colledge and McGinn, p. 294.

[2] *Eckhart,* Colledge and McGinn, p. 287.

[3] *Maximus,* p. 39.

[4] *Maximus,* pp. 59-60.

[5] *Eckhart,* Colledge and McGinn, p. 250.

[6] *Eckhart,* Colledge and McGinn, p. 288.

[7] *Angelus Silesius: The Cherubinic Wanderer,* tr. Maria Shrady (New York: Paulist, 1986), p. 46.

[8] *Eckhart,* Colledge and McGinn, p. 252.

[9] *Maximus,* p. 50.

[10] *Maximus,* p. 58.

[11] *Maximus,* p. 75.

[12] *Eckhart,* Colledge and McGinn, p. 251.

[13] Gregory, p. 283.

[14] Grace M. Jantzen, *Julian of Norwich* (New York: Paulist, 1988), p. 91.

[15] *Julian,* p. 135.

[16] *Julian,* p. 140.

[17] Gregory, p. 238.

[18] *Bonaventure,* p. 59.

[19] *Julian,* p. 137.

[20] *Julian,* p. 115.

[21] Gregory, p. 225.

[22] *Eckhart,* Colledge and McGinn, p. 267.

[23] Gregory, p. 114.

[24] *Bernard,* p. 176.

[25] *Bernard,* p. 177.

[26] *Julian,* p. 93.

[27] *Julian,* p. 160.

[28] *Catherine of Siena: The Dialogue,* tr. Suzanne Noffke, O.P. (New York: Paulist, 1980), p. 29.

[29] *Evagrius Ponticus: The Praktikos and Chapters on Prayer,* tr. John Eudes Bamberger, O.C.S.O. (Kalamazoo, MI: Cistercian, 1978), pp. 29-30.

[30] *Catherine,* p. 158.

[31] *Catherine,* p. 88.

[32] *Catherine,* p. 48.

[33] *Eckhart,* Colledge and McGinn, p. 251.

[34] *Sayings of the Desert Fathers,* tr. Benedicta Ward, S.L.G. (Kalamazoo, MI: Cistercian, 1978), p. 2.

[35] *Sayings,* p. 89.

[36] *Bernard,* p. 227.

[37] *Birgitta,* p. 104.

[38] *Sayings,* p. 144.

[39] *Sayings,* pp. 195-196.

[40] *Evagrius,* pp. 33-34.

[41] *Sayings,* p. 29.

[42] *Sayings,* p. 88.

[43] *Sayings,* p. 187.

[44] *The Cloud of Unknowing,* ed. William Johnston (Garden City, NY: Doubleday Image, 1973), p. 55.

[45] *Cloud,* p. 56.

[46] *Maximus,* p. 61.

[47] *Evagrius,* p. 75.

[48] *Eckhart,* Colledge and McGinn, p. 277.

[49] *Eckhart,* p. 179.

[50] *Symeon the New Theologian: The Discourses,* tr. C.J. deCatanzaro (New York: Paulist, 1980), p. 237.

Attitudes to Be Cultivated

T he spiritual life is essentially interior. The full inner life overflows and expresses itself in the externals of our living. The inner uses external support as well. This principle of interiority is the chief truth that tells us that our state in life does not determine whether we can enjoy union with God. Every person in every circumstance can develop an inner life with God, deep in the heart and clear in the consciousness.

As Angelus says in one of his amazing couplets: "If you do not Paradise first in yourself possess, / Believe me that you never will find to it access."[1] So we make our effort to cooperate with God's grace by beginning to practice within ourselves, where everything counts.

We may find that notion problematic if we have assumed that our inner life is not under our control, bandied around as it is by circumstances. That assumption is false. We have vast powers, conscious and unconscious, over our interior situation.

An old story (updated in the following version) is a perfect example:

A couple went on vacation to an expensive hotel on a Caribbean island. They were looking for quiet and sunshine and had been assured that they would find both in this beautiful place. But the second evening they were there, they began to hear an unwelcome sound in the next room. Someone was practicing on a violin—the same phrase over and over again until our couple was nearly frantic. Then scales, up and down, up and down—a new key and more scales, up and down. Then that same phrase again and again and...

Finally, they could bear it no longer. The man roared down to the manager and demanded to have the person in the next room silenced or moved. The manager listened quietly, then thought for a moment.

"I'm very sorry, sir, that you have been disturbed. I will be happy to have our staff move you and your wife to another room, but I truly cannot move your neighbor. You see, it is Itzhak Perlman who is practicing there."

Shortly, our couple were delightedly inviting their vacation acquaintances to their suite for refreshments and to listen to the great violinist practice.

A lasting change of attitude may not occur as quickly as that. It may take time and effort, but it is always well within our reach.

If we sincerely desire God, it will soon enough become evident that inside changes are called for. After all, the journey is a transformation, a change into what is presently beyond us, but can become our own: a life united to Christ in God.

A good place to begin to practice is with our attitudes.

Attitudes are inner states, positions, stances. They are much more than thoughts or emotions. Attitudes tend to pervade many aspects of our life; they are habitual and often based on assumptions we have not yet examined. Attitudes are like filters through which we experience every aspect of our life.

Our attitudes can serve our spiritual life or they can impede it. We want to choose those which help us. Attitudes consistent with growing toward God in our heart have been called "virtues." Mystics from the earliest days in Christianity have urged us to "practice the virtues." Maximus says that "through the virtues," deification takes place.[2] Gregory understands it in terms of the Image of God within: "When

God made you, He at once endowed your nature with this perfection...an imitation of the perfections of His own nature.... You must then wash away, by a life of virtue, the dirt that has come to cling to your heart like plaster, and then your divine beauty will once again shine forth."[3]

Later, the notion of practicing the virtues became systematized, and lists of the virtues were made, seven of which ended up in the *Baltimore Catechism.* You may even have memorized them.

The trouble with the lists is not that they were wrong but that they gathered a sense of obligation as the centuries went by. As we have seen, no one is obligated to the highest life in God, so we are not obliged to alter our attitudes or, to put it another way, to develop inner virtues. In an effort to avoid the moralistic view of "virtues," we will call them attitudes, except when quoting our saints. When our experts say "virtues," we will understand "attitudes."

Negative attitudes are interior realities that actually hinder the work of the Spirit in us. They contract or even close our heart so we cannot receive the Lord. When we practice virtuous attitudes we "actually participate in God Himself," as Gregory says.[4] Maximus is even more explicit. In "the qualities of the virtues...God continually becomes man. As His body he has the qualities of the virtues."[5] So in the cultivation of good attitudes, we not only open our heart to receive the Lord but are made to be like him.

By our attitudes, then, we decide for or against the action of the Lord within us, not because of worthiness as such but because it is in the nature of creation.

All our existing attitudes are so habitual we may hardly be aware of them. They are stances, present and effective before we see them. In the instant we recognize an attitude, we must choose to change it if it closes us to God or to keep and encourage it if it is an open-hearted attitude. Both choices require grace. We will beg God for his help.

The choices we make will reflect what we most deeply want. "The aim of the life of virtue is to become like God," Gregory says, "...so that the form of transcendent Being might be revealed in them."[6] How beautiful it sounds!

Let's survey some attitudes known to be Christlike. We can practice them, choose *for* them, and develop them. Some may be ours
already. The following choices do not pretend to be complete, but if
we choose one or two of them for consistent practice, all others
required will come to awareness in the right time. The Holy Spirit
guides our process to its completion.

Where we start is up to us. As Angelus says, "The virtues are
together so closely intertwined, / That he who one possesses may all
the others find."[7] I suggest starting with one or two that are attractive,
that you may enjoy exploring, and that will come up often enough in
your daily life to give you lots of opportunities to practice.

In general, one may work well with all attitudes by taking these
steps:

1. Pray for God's grace and help.
2. Be willing to change and to see yourself as "in process."
3. Keep track of what helps, be ready to drop what does not help.
4. In all efforts, give thanks.

DEEPENING OUR DESIRE, YEARNING,
AND LOVE FOR GOD

We yearn for God, some of us a little, some passionately, some
totally. Our yearning empowers our journey, always wanting more of
God, always loving God more, desiring God more intensely. Some
people's experience is that their desire for God does all the work: they
yearn for God so deeply that everything else seems to come almost
of itself. Yearning for God is sheer power. It becomes a basic stance
in many lives.

The *Cloud* tells us, "If you wish to keep growing you must nourish
in your heart the lively longing for God."[8] How can we encourage this
attitude? God can be counted on to help deepen our longing, but what
is our part?

Suggestions for nourishing our yearning follow.

Pray

First, we may pray over and over again, with Bernard, "How I pray that that burning desire and longing in the hearts of these holy men of old may be aroused in me."[9] Let us pester God constantly with this prayer!

Feed on the Scriptures

We continue with Scripture reading. "Here the words of life are offered to you, which make those who feed on them immortal!"[10] If we are to "feed on" Scripture, reflective reading is best. The gospels stimulate our knowledge of Christ and our longing for him. The Psalms are much loved. So are the Letters of Paul. Some people select verses from the Mass reading for the day, others take readings from the Liturgy of the Hours. We can select the parts of Scripture that most appeal to us.

When we read the Bible to nourish our God-hunger, we want to read slowly in a relaxed and leisurely way, pausing whenever a word or phrase awakens a response in our heart. The Lord is present in the sacred Word, so we can converse with him, enjoy the beauty before our mind, savor everything about the whole experience. This is an ancient and well-loved form of prayer because it becomes an encounter with Christ, the Living Word.

All the mystical writers show evidence of being so immersed in Scripture that their vocabulary and style of expression echo it. They quote Scripture as part of their natural writing or speech, as demonstrated in recorded sermons or other talks. They do not always admonish their hearers to absorb their minds in the Scripture, only because they assume it is being done wherever possible. They are themselves the bright example of the benefit of scriptural reading. They often wrote mystical commentaries on portions of the Bible. Some examples are Bernard's on the Song of Songs, Gregory on Moses' life, Bonaventure on the creation stories.

The more we know the Scripture, the more we will know about
God and the more we will meet God in it. And God is so fascinating
that the more we meet him, the more of God our heart desires. Our
yearning will grow and become an ever stronger motivation for every
effort we make to cooperate with God's grace. Finally, we may
experience with Gregory that those who know "the secret mysteries
of this book...[will] be substantially transformed by Christ's word
into something divine."[11]

Practice Contemplation

We may nourish our longing for God by practicing some form of
contemplative prayer. It is best to do it daily, but any time at all is
better than none at all. This form of prayer is like a child's learning
to walk. At first, God may give new and wonderful experiences of his
presence in love, in the heart. As our practice continues, God may
withdraw these experiences. Then we will yearn for him even more
than before. We have tasted and seen how good the Lord is (Psalm
34:9) and now we want more of him.

The Lord speaks in Catherine's *Dialogue,* saying, "To exercise
them...I take back my spiritual comfort and let them experience
struggles...and though I may take away their comfort, I do not take
away grace."[12] God never leaves. God sometimes merely hides our
experience of him so that we may long for him the more, seek him
the more, love him more in our struggle than perhaps we tend to in
our comfort. Yet God is always there, deepening our desire for him,
supporting our effort, and preparing to reward it with himself in his
own time. Ours it is to keep praying.

Seek God's Will in All Things

If we desire God, we also basically desire God's will. We want
those we love to have what they want, don't we? It's the same with

God, except that when God wants something, we know for sure it is good. Eckhart tells us that every good man will "will what is the particular will of God, for it is impossible for God to will anything but good...and what is more, it is the best."[13] So we can want God's will in total confidence.

As we seek God's will in all circumstances, we long even more for God himself. We may not receive a direct answer about God's will for every single decision we must make. Yet our effort to seek God's will and our remembering to ask God about everything will increase our desire for ever closer union with God, until our wills are totally unified with God's will. We want our love for God and our longing for that union to increase until there is no space in us for anything but God.

Remember God

Finally, we nourish our longing for God by remembering him as constantly as we possibly can. Birgitta hears God say that this is his intention for us: "I gave man a heart so that he might enclose in it me, his God...so that his delight might be in thinking of me."[14]

In the beginning, of course, we will remember God only sporadically, in the blank spots of our days. We can fill our environment with reminders—symbols, words, pictures, music—and we can pray for grace to recall the presence of God more and more often. Our remembering gradually grows into praying without ceasing, as Paul admonished the first Christians to practice. (See 1 Thessalonians 5:17.)

Remembering God is a way of cherishing God, of dreaming about him, of wishing that we were totally present to him all the time. We remember what we love.

> Sailors speak of the sea, the hunters of their hounds,
> The miser speaks of gold, the soldier of his wounds.
> Me, since I am in love, nothing so much befits
> As having God and love forever on my lips.[15]

Every time we do remember God, we will likely be aware that for the just-past hour or half-day or whatever, we have forgotten God. We will alternate between remembering God and forgetting. Out of the sweetness of remembering and still knowing our forgetfulness, we will want God more. Our yearning is intensified—our prayer is being answered.

So with Gregory, "Fixing our eyes on those things which help us to see [God], we must ever keep alive in us the desire to see more and more. And so no limit can be set to our progress towards God."[16]

TRUST AND CONTENTMENT

We humans usually imagine that a contented heart is the result of getting everything we want. If only all our desires were filled, we would be content. This is not true. As we saw in "General Principles of Spiritual Life," desire has a life of its own. On its own, desire will never stop but finds new objects as time goes on.

Birgitta tells of a vision in which she saw an acquaintance, now dead, who begged her for prayers. The acquaintance was being held back from blessedness by "the fact that I was not content with the things that I had, but wanted always to have more."[17] Whether it happens in heaven, I cannot say, but it definitely happens in our daily life; happiness is pushed away by our discontent. So is God.

Contentment is an attitude we can practice, though full contentment is a spiritual gift from God. For that we can pray often and heartily.

Contentment is based on trust in God. Eckhart recommends trust, "for everything that we dare trust to be in God we find in him truly and a thousand times more...no man could ever trust him too much. Nothing that a man can do is so fitting as to have great trust in God. God never ceased to achieve great things through those who ever gained great confidence in him."[18]

Like all attitudes, contentment can become habitual. Until that happens, however, it is not easy to gain contentment by decision. To strengthen our contentment, we can remind ourselves that God always gives us, who long to know his life and love in our own heart, what we actually need in every moment. Where we are right now, in exactly the condition of this instant, we have what we need *for this moment.*

When Birgitta was asked by the Lord to travel to the Holy Land—a frightful undertaking in her day—she objected. He replied to her, "Who is the Establisher of nature? Is it not I? Therefore I will increase your strength. I will provide for the way. I will guide you and lead you back."[19] Words to remember well in our smaller, daily experiences.

Discontent arises often from one of two other attitudinal habits, neither one useful to spiritual life. One is desire or fear projected into the unknown future. We all do it. It does not help, however, because it is not the truth. In no way can we ever predict our circumstances next year—not even next week or next hour. A phone call could change everything in a flash.

There are no guarantees, except one: God will never abandon us and will always give us what we truly need. The Hebrews heard it from the Lord in their exile: "Can a mother forget her infant, be without tenderness for the child of her womb? Even should she forget, I will never forget you. See, upon the palms of my hands I have written your name" (Isaiah 49:15-16).

We may not always think our needs are what God thinks they are. If we trust that God knows more about our life than we do, then we will be ready to wait confidently for what we do not yet see. Then we will remember that God always gives what we truly need for growth toward union with him. Then we can be content for this moment; it is truly quite full enough.

The second source of discontent is comparing ourselves to others. This tendency can invade even our spiritual lives. We may see someone who progresses faster than we do, who had the wonderful experiences of the Lord that we want, or who seems to have it "all together." It can be subtle, this comparison.

The best advice is "Stop comparing." Every time we find ourselves comparing, we can remind ourselves that God knows what is best for us and gives it to us. We agree that this very present circumstance *is*

God's will for us, and we relax into spiritual contentment. Let the desires rage away! They are not forever. A contented heart is forever.

The only useful disturbance of our contentment is an inner remorse for our failings and wrongs. This is not the same as feeling guilty. It is rather a real sorrow, an honest shame.

Symeon the New Theologian urges a daily contact with this sorrow, a repeated renewal of it, because it is cleansing. "When...this unceasing penitence is pursued...it gradually causes us to shed bitter tears and by these wipes away and cleanses the filth and defilement of the soul....Afterwards it produces...increasing joy in our hearts and enables us to see the radiance that never sets."[20]

I can testify that remorse is cleansing. It burns like fire and consumes all the deadness around it.

Once a mentor whom I loved and respected, especially for his spiritual awareness, asked me a question about myself. It was a small question, but I knew immediately that the true answer would show me to be less than I wanted this man to think I was. So instantly, I lied. He accepted it, and we continued to talk. Only later, when I was driving alone on a freeway, did I become fully conscious of the lie. Shame flooded my heart; I felt fire from my toes to my scalp.

Why had I done it? Ego, of course, but it was so unnecessary. I did know better, and I had violated my own longing for God. There was no excuse, though my mind tried hard to shrug it off. But the God-given remorse in my heart told me that after a certain point in spiritual life, there is no such thing as a small matter.

In the midst of the fire of remorse, I turned to God and begged forgiveness with my whole being. Of course, it was given. From that experience of remorse, some aspects of my relationship with God were made permanently better. I was cleaner within; God was dearer than ever.

I have often returned to that remorse, not to whip myself for the lie (which is decidedly unhealthy) but to recall my weakness and God's love and mercy. Heaven knows, I've done things far worse than that, and I try to gather them all under this awareness of remorse and mercy. It helps. It somehow puts my perspective right again. I become content with my circumstances but not complacent about my inner need.

Eckhart approves this combination. "You should be content with all creatures who are under God, but you should never be content with God....The more you have of God, the more you long for him."[21]

DEVOTION AND SELF-GIVING

Devotion is the warmth of our love for God. The more we receive from God, the more devotion we experience. The more we express our devotion, the more it grows inside. The more devotion we have, the more we love God and the more open we are to receive more of God. It is a wonderful circle of loving openness.

What do we mean by devotion? Well, what is a devoted parent? This mother or father loves the child, keeps an eye on the child, cares for the child constantly, enjoys the child, wants the best for him or her, builds a life around the child's welfare. This quality of love that centers a life around the object of devotion is what we mean when we speak of devotion to God.

The devoted disciple loves the Lord and keeps an inner eye attentive to the Lord. The devoted disciple wants what God wants, cares for the people God cares for, designs his or her life around the Lord.

Since devotion has a warm emotional quality, it begs for expression. As we express our devotion to God, it grows. *How* we express it does not matter so much, but we cooperate with God in our heart when we do express it. We may look for small expressions at first, seen only by the Lord: a moment's extra pause when we genuflect, invisible to others but enough to let our heart bow, too; lighting a candle at home as a prayer for our day; putting a picture of Jesus in our place of work (even if we think we have to hide it in a frequently opened desk drawer!); singing a hymn to God; making up a poem for the Lord and reading it aloud to him. If we look for simple, honest expressions of our love for God, we will find myriads of them.

One such expression is offering each of our activities to the Lord, one at a time. To make such an offering of our day, first thing in the morning, is lovely. How much more lovely to remember to offer each task to God as we begin it: each enjoyment, each bit of recreation, each conversation, each moment of lovemaking, each errand, each trip to town, each red light, each green light—everything! A day like this is a day full of devotion to God, filled with God in the heart.

Such a day makes us want another day as full of God, so we do it again. When offering our activities becomes habitual, we may take the next step and offer our emotions, every single emotional reaction we experience. This will be harder to remember, but it gives rise to a more intimate experience of devotion to God. God is likely to take away the negative offerings of emotion and increase the beautiful ones, thus showing us the Lord's devotion to the disciple. Offering becomes an exchange of inner gifts. Who would not be devoted to such a Lord?

When emotions are regularly offered to God, the next step is offering our thoughts as we are aware of them. With this offering, the fabric of our mental experience will begin to be molded by the loving Lord. Nothing will ever be the same: we will become devotion itself, moment to moment, and we will love God and rejoice in God. "A burning devotion to God discovers renewal and refreshment in him as at the touch of his hand."[22]

That is the purpose of devotion, which is its own reason for being. In the end, love is for love; devotion is just for devotion. Once tasted, we wouldn't want for a moment to return to life without devotion and self-offering.

RECOVERING A SENSE OF THE SACRED

One of the tragedies of modern American life is that we have lost touch with an awareness of sacredness. We think it is natural to be cool, to be unawed by anything. We take everything for granted and hasten off to the next novelty. We allow ourselves little time to wonder at anything at all, because it seems to our society that we have conquered it all. How much interior richness we have lost!

We miss the sacred because we do not know God, but we also miss God because we have forgotten to be aware of the sacred in our lives.

Hildegard of Bingen was vividly aware of the holiness of all creation. In one of her astounding visions, the Creator speaks:

> I, the highest and fiery power, have kindled every spark of life, and I emit nothing that is deadly. I decide on all reality. With my lofty wings I fly above the globe. With wisdom I have rightly put the universe in order. I, the fiery life of divine essence, am aflame beyond the beauty of the meadows. I gleam in the waters. I burn in the sun, moon and stars. With every breeze, as with invisible life that contains everything, I awaken everything to life.[23]

There was a time in the memory of any Catholic over the age of thirty-five when a church was a sacred place, the sanctuary even more sacred, and the holy vessels more sacred still. A church was a place of awareness of the holy, of awe and wonder at the mystery of God with us.

Yet it was not the dim lights or the communion rail that created this awareness of sacredness. It was something we brought with us to the church; it was a sacred attitude. In reality, there is nothing profane or secular; everything is sacred. There is only a secular attitude. Ours has become a secular attitude.

In themselves, all things, all places, and all people are sacred because they are creations of God. Hildegard saw that "God has composed the world out of its elements for the glory of his name. He has strengthened it with the winds, bound and illuminated it with the stars, and filled it with the other creatures....Out of the original source of the true Love in whose knowledge the cosmic wheel rests, there shines forth an exceedingly precise order over all things."[24]

We know a lot about things, even about people, but we do not know how things come into being and go out of being once again. That is God's. For us, it is mystery. "The all-powerful and unutterable God, who was before ages but did not have a beginning nor will ever have an end, formed every creature in a wonderful manner with the creative power of willing and then placed every creature in a wondrous manner. How did God do this?"[25] Are we awed by it?

In contrast to Hildegard, we moderns tend to see everything through secular-colored glasses, as if God were not real. The tragedy for our spiritual lives is that God could speak to our heart in everything around us, in every place and in every person. We miss his speech because we have decided (without really deciding) that everything is ordinary and outside of God.

We can recover the sense of the sacred. We can practice a sacred inner attitude. We may have to talk to ourselves and seek the sacred quite deliberately at first. We can begin by recalling moments that have been truly sacred to us: the birth of our baby, an unexpected healing, a phenomenon in nature, a childhood experience when we knew instinctively that living was sacred. What was the awareness in our heart like in that precious moment? Can we rekindle it? Pause right now in your reading and remember how it was...

I recommend the following exercises to be done with open and prayerful heart. Ask the Lord to show you the sacredness of all his creation, then try one of these experiments:

- ♦ Before a meal, ponder how the food on your table got there—not just from the store but before that, all the way back to the seed, the farmer, the soil, and the rain. Let your heart say a silent "Wow."
- ♦ Some night about two a.m., when the sky is clear, go outside and let the stars and the moon talk to you about their Creator.
- ♦ Cup a flower in both your hands without breaking its stem and look at it with love. Listen with your heart.
- ♦ When making love, pause inwardly a moment to marvel at the intricacies of the human body and the exquisiteness of its creation.
- ♦ Spend a few minutes gazing with an open heart at your sleeping child.

♦ Take in your hands something you handle all the time—a tool, a dish, a piece of clothing, a pen—and really look at it, reflecting on all that went into its design, its production, its materials, its original idea. Wonder at it and its uses to you.

♦ Look into the face of another human being, loved or unknown, and marvel at the miracle that human life is.

♦ Go into a church, preferably empty and unfamiliar (if it is usually locked, go early before services), and sit quietly, waiting for God. Do the same with a favorite spot in nature.

You get the idea. You can find many simple and available occasions to open your heart to wonder, to recover the sense of the sacred in all things. Nurture it. Make it an attitude that pervades your days and all you do. Each morning on awakening, recall your sacred attitude and choose it consciously. Let your heart fill with wonder and only then open your eyes.

We may have thought we have to go to a special place to find the sacred. No, we need only open the heart to a truer way of seeing, a way of recognizing the divine Lord in all the world, in all our life, in ourselves. If we look for it, ordinary life will give us back the sacred because it is true.

Sometimes when we have enjoyed close communion with the Lord, we may find that the world appears different to us, alive and incalculably precious. That is a sense of the sacred awakened by our conscious contact with the Most Sacred, who is God. Ultimately, our loving contact with God will awaken our awareness of the sacred dimension of all that is, and life will become spontaneously warm and wonder-filled. And in our times of prayer, God will seem more available to our opened heart.

REJOICING IN ALL GOODNESS

Devotion and wonder naturally open the way to rejoicing in everything that is beautiful and good. If we can recapture our awareness of the sacredness of everything, with Hildegard, we will also see with her that "all of creation is a symphony of joy and jubilation."[26]

Rejoicing is easy when the beautiful and good have come to us. When this happens, we can enhance our rejoicing by making it as conscious as possible, prolonging it a little, and turning it into prayer. Rejoice to the Lord, rejoice with the Lord, whenever anything appears that is wonderful.

Rejoicing may not come quite as easily when the beautiful and good happen to someone else—especially if that person received something we wanted for ourselves. In these circumstances, we may have to make a conscious choice to rejoice with the other. Our emotions may not go along with our choice at first. Let's rejoice with the lottery winners! It's the observation of Evagrius that "happy is the [one] who views the welfare and progress of all men with as much joy as if it were his own."[27] Joy is its own reward, and consistently choosing it will align our emotions with reality.

Choose to revel before God in everything that is good. It is too easy to take the good for granted, then complain about the less than good. Reveling in the lovely will help us to stop complaining. It will help us to be happy. Happiness in goodness promotes goodness and hence more happiness, and so on.

Julian sees rejoicing as a foretaste of heaven. "I saw [Jesus] reign in his house as a king and fill it all full of joy and mirth, gladdening and consoling his dear friends with himself, very familiarly and courteously...in endless love...fill[ing] all heaven full of the joy and bliss of the divinity."[28]

Why is rejoicing good for spiritual life? Because it opens the heart and draws us nearer to Christ. Julian says, "Glad and merry and sweet is the blessed and lovely demeanor of our Lord towards our souls, for he saw us always living in love-longing, and he wants our souls to be gladly disposed...and he lifts up and will draw our outer disposition to our inward, and will make us all at unity with him...in the lasting joy which is Jesus."[29] An open heart is a heart capable of receiving divine love, of giving love, and then of becoming love.

When rejoicing becomes a prayer, as it will if we are trying to remember God and offer every moment to him, our joy turns into gratitude and praise. Benedictine Brother David Steindl-Rast believes that gratitude is the core of all true prayer, vital to everyone's relationship with the Lord.

As our spiritual life deepens, gratitude deepens, too. It becomes praise of God for God's own sake. As we practice praising God for himself, we are filled with rejoicing. Then everything seems good to us, because we find God in all. Rejoicing and praising not only support our love for God, they are an expression of our love for God and an acknowledgment of God's love for us. "Always, the more delight and joy that we accept…with reverence and humility, the more pleasing it is to God."[30]

So rejoicing becomes more than an attitude that helps us find God. It becomes the very nature of our relationship with God, the quality of that union we seek.

In the beginning, we practice by choosing to rejoice *with* God, if only for a moment, over every good event that comes along. Even if it is only a whispered "Wow, Lord, that was beautiful—hurray!" If we do it every time, we soon will fill our days with awareness of the goodness of the life God has given us, and God will have found a deeper dwelling in our heart, in the very space where all the complaining used to be!

HUMILITY AND WILLINGNESS

Humility is a necessary attitude but too profound to be more than touched upon in these pages. It has been discussed by saints for centuries, and I recommend that every reader make a deeper study of it. Humility is foundational and a mark of greatness in God. It is not usual; yet it is available to us.

For a modern insight into humility, I am indebted to Robert Fritz (founder of Technologies for Creating), who talks about the difference between the attitudes of the *performer* and those of the *learner*.

The *performer* in life wants to be seen, wants to be right—or thinks

he or she *has* to be right. The performer tries to have it all together
and to let other people know it. The performer is trying to prove
something, perhaps quite subtly. All this is detrimental to spiritual
life. It is a hard attitude, a closed and defensive attitude. We have
come by it quite honestly, since we are usually more rewarded for our
performance than for learning. Nevertheless, it leads to an inability
to be humble.

The *learner,* on the other hand, is primarily interested in growing
in any situation and from any person. The learner asks questions
instead of giving advice, wants to understand more than to explain,
recognizes that mistakes are good teachers so is comfortable making
them, and is relaxed and open rather than tense and closed. This
learner-stance is itself a humble position, leading to humility.

We can choose to think as learners, behave as learners, and become
God's learners if we wish. It may require some attention at first, but
it is not terribly difficult.

Humility is, as Bernard says, "the virtue by which a man recognizes
his own unworthiness because he really knows himself."[31] It may feel
a little scary at first because it knocks us off our prideful perch. But
we already know that emotions do not tell us the truth, don't we?

Another facet of humility, and an attitude that goes along with
being God's learner, is willingness. Gerald May (a psychiatrist and
the director of Shalem Institute for Spirituality) has said that willingness is the essential attitude for the spiritual life: willingness to be
taught, willingness to be opened, willingness to be loved, willingness
to obey God's guidance and to accept God's gifts.

The opposite of willingness is willfulness that insists on its own
way, be it subtle or painfully obvious.

We can practice willingness by saying an inner yes to whatever
happens. "I shall always be completely consoled and joyful, at all
times and under all circumstances....If God wills to give what I ask
for, I thereby have it and rejoice; and if God does not will to give it,
[I] accept that I lack it in the same will of God," Eckhart writes.[32]

He means, "Okay, Lord, I'm willing to live with this for you, to
love this one for you, to accept this gift from you." We can practice

this at any time, in any place. It is probably most useful to practice it in those situations that are not to our immediate liking or that have no ego-benefits in them.

God tells Catherine that "I want [the soul] to be humble, to see that of herself she is nothing, and to recognize that her existence and every gift beyond that comes from me, that I am her life."[33]

Such humility is an essential attitude in spiritual growth because we can really know union with God only on God's terms. It's not that God is a tyrant but that we don't know what we are about! Catherine reminds us that we often find ourselves unable to be as good as we like and then the soul "is humbled in true self-knowledge, and in the light of holy faith she runs to me, God eternal."[34] By being willing contentedly to go along with the Lord in the circumstances of our lives, we can discover what it means to be one with the Lord in the heart.

The learner before God is willing to listen and willing to obey. We also can practice listening to one another. That will teach us how to listen to God, because God does use life's events to teach us as well as to give us direct guidance sometimes. We can practice being learners willingly, being obedient willingly, and listening willingly to God in every situation and every moment. Then we will be more able to hear God directly in our prayer, in our heart, for we will be more "like your Maker and your God, by humbling yourself with your brethren."[35]

Encouraging and lovely is the view of humility held by the anonymous author of the *Cloud.* He said that self-knowledge is one motive for humility but that there is a better one: "God's goodness and love...will keep us humble."[36] Indeed, who among us has not known a moment of humility when we recognize that we are divinely, eternally loved?

SEEING GOD IN ALL PEOPLE

A minister and professor once wrote to me that one of his most rewarding spiritual efforts is to see the Image of God in every human face. He experiences today what Gregory taught sixteen centuries ago: God "dwells within you, nor is He cramped as He pervades your entire being, saying: I will dwell in them and walk among them."[37]

When we perceive in another human being the Image of God shining forth, it is not something made up. In that moment, we are seeing the Truth. Every human being *is* the Image of God, the creation of God, the beloved of the Lord. No exceptions. Evagrius knew it and saw its effects: "Happy is the [one] who considers all men as god— after God."[38]

Yet we often do not perceive God in everyone. We see people who are better than ourselves or worse, people who are being nice or being nasty, people who are helping us or in our way, people our society has taught us to be distrustful and afraid of. We usually see other people in relation to our own interests. It is an ego-centric position. It affects our relationships and hampers our readiness to know God.

Why do we not see God's face in every face? One hindrance is simply that we usually are not looking for God when we look at others. God is not hard to perceive when we actually look at another from our heart. We are often unacquainted with the Image of God in ourselves, and as a result, it is harder to find elsewhere. This works both ways. As we discover the Lord shining in our own heart, we will see him more easily in others. Likewise, as we perceive God's presence in our neighbors, we will find him more easily within ourselves. Eckhart reminds us that "truly you are the hidden God, in the ground of the soul, where God's ground and the soul's ground are one."[39] It is true of all.

For practice with this change in attitude and perception, here are two suggestions:

First, we make the effort to remind ourselves to look for the Lord in every human face. Begin where it is easiest, perhaps in the faces of those we dearly love. Then we may turn our attention to the faces of acquaintances, then to strangers. The whole experience of a bus ride or a traffic jam changes when each face is the face of God to us. Finally, we may seek the face of God in those we dislike or who have hurt or ignored us. God is just as much there, but we may be a little blinder in that direction. Practice and prayer will help.

It takes only a moment to ask: "Where is God in this face?" In a second, we can let the heart look through our eyes—and there is God looking back at us!

Another vital practice is to stop finding fault with other people. "They said of Abba Macarius the Great [Evagrius' teacher] that he became…a god upon earth, because, just as God protects the world, so Abba Macarius would cover the faults which he saw, as though he did not see them; and those which he heard, as though he did not hear them."[40]

It's hard to see God in a person we are busily criticizing. Until we begin to try this deliberately, few of us realize how much of our thinking and conversation is taken up with faultfinding. Think about your last three conversations; they will show you how to practice.

At first, we can simply close our mouth so as not to say aloud the thoughts in our mind. That will change the character of our conversation. A temptation that arises at this stage is that our partners in conversation will probably not be practicing seeing God in others, and we will want to find fault with them for finding fault with others. The antidote to this is to remember to see God in the person with whom we are talking.

The next step is to practice in our thinking. Here we can replace every critical thought with a thought about the person's lovely qualities, and this thought will be strengthened if we say it aloud.

Eventually, we simply will not see faults. We will be like Abba Poemen of the Desert Fathers. Some others came to see him and asked if they should reprove the brothers who slept during the Liturgy of the Hours. Abba Poemen replied, "Actually, if I saw a brother sleeping, I would put his head on my knees and let him rest."[41]

If you can find a friend or family member to be your partner in this practice, it will be a wonderful support. If you and someone you often talk with agree that your conversation will omit faultfinding—and persist in it—your attitude toward other people will never be the same. You will begin to experience God where before you saw only faults.

KINDNESS AND GENEROSITY

As we begin more and more to see God in others, we begin to see people as God sees them: lovable and lovely. It is then natural to be kind to others, to want only good for them, to treat them gently.

We love the Lord. If the Lord was suffering right before our eyes, or even if he were behaving in a way we did not understand, wouldn't we be compassionate before our thoughts turned ugly?

Simple kindness to others can become the whole of a person's spiritual discipline. It is not always easy, although the more we see God in others, the easier it is to be kindly. Yes, it often requires self-restraint, especially if in the moment our emotions are not kind.

Bernard suggests that we think "how easily you are tempted, how prone you are to sin, how easily you let yourself off, and so hasten to help others in a spirit of gentleness."[42] So if our deep intention is to become kind, we can practice acting gently no matter what our emotions are doing.

In this, as in other attitudinal practices, we can begin deliberately with people who do not seem to make difficulties for us. But eventually, a challenge will come.

Once a man was notified that he would have to share his office with the most difficult coworker in the department. He resisted mightily, but there was no way out of it. Then he remembered that God lived in this coworker and decided to treat him accordingly. So he smothered the coworker with kindness, putting aside his own preferences and doing things as the coworker liked. He did this not as a victim who was too weak to do otherwise but as master of himself, strong enough to be generous. The outcome was predictable: no matter how the coworker behaved, the kind one lived in joy and love, for he saw God with him in the office.

The ultimate in kindness and generosity of heart is forgiveness. To be kind and generous to one who has hurt us (or others) is a vital and powerful practice. When we begin it, *as a practice,* we soon may find that something in us likes being angry or resentful or hurt. It is that selfishness in ourselves we must battle.

The best antidote for anger is forgiveness, offered because we know that deep in every person is the Lord. Being in touch with this truth, we may feel compassion for the hurtful person, knowing that he or she is also in pain and ignorance; otherwise, no hurt would have been done. In compassion, forgiveness is not debated, because it is already there.

We can become, if we wish, more like Abba Moses in the desert long ago. Once the brothers were holding a council about the faults of one of them. At first, Abba Moses refused to go, but the others insisted. "So he got up and went. He took a leaking jug filled with water and carried it with him. The others came out to meet him and said to him, 'What is this, Father?' The old man said to them, 'My sins run out behind me, and I do not see them, and today I am coming to judge the errors of another.' When they heard that, they said no more to the brother, but forgave him."[43]

Forgiving is the most victorious act we can perform. It is a profound choice of kindness above all, no matter what we think has been done wrong. It is God's own act, as we know from our own experience. It makes us more like Christ, who forgave his killers.

An accessible practice toward forgiveness is to recall that the Image of God lives in our personal "enemies" as much as God lives in our own heart. We can remind ourselves, too, that pain (however inflicted) is neutral until it is attached to our negative emotional tendencies; only then does our anger flare. A college friend used to work in a mental hospital, where she was often hit—and it hurt! But she was there because of her compassion for these people, and so anger did not arise.

So it is with God. God not only forgives specific acts. God lives, as it were, with a constantly forgiving heart because God is pure compassion. There is not the slightest retention of our faults in God's knowledge of us; they are forgiven before our next breath. By sharing God's forgiveness with one another, we become sisters and brothers on this planet of God's.

EQUANIMITY

The practices just discussed affect our overall attitude. Little by little, we discover new serenity of mind. We may notice that irritation does not arise as quickly, or sometimes not at all, in situations where it used to. We may smile at events that used to upset us with anxieties or resentments. "There is no difference," says Angelus Silesius, "should they the dung be raking, / Angels like it no less than rest and music-making."[44]

We may discover one day that our general emotional tone is easier, lighter, calmer. It indicates the beginning of equanimity. Equanimity is a state in which experiencing God is easier and more nearly constant.

Full equanimity of mind and emotion means that nothing affects us, nothing disturbs our peaceful and joyous experience of life. When we have pleasures, we enjoy them and delight in them, but we aren't as excited over them as before. When we have pain or sufferings, we feel them, but they do not trouble us or upset us as they once did. If we enjoy equanimity, when people praise us, we take it only for what it is—a human opinion. It means little to us. When people find fault with us, we take it only for what it is—a human opinion. It means little to us.

Moreover, not only events but thoughts about them will not matter to the person of equanimity, for he or she "is not disturbed by changing events, but...remains unmoved at the memory of them as well."[45]

Whew, you may be thinking, *that sounds impossible! I'm not even sure I like it.*

Equanimity is not indifference, cut off from life and making our days tasteless. It is the subsidence of ego-domination, and it allows us to experience everything without being upset *about ourselves.* Of course, if one prefers inner turmoil, equanimity will not seem attractive. But one does not know God in the midst of turmoil. One knows God in interior peacefulness and joyfulness, regardless of what is going on externally.

It was from the profound equanimity of love that Jesus was able to forgive his killers and take care of Mary from the cross. It was from profound equanimity that Sir Thomas More, when he was about to be beheaded, jokingly asked the executioner to spare his beard.

No matter what, "contempt, it may be, just as respect; bitterness just as sweetness; the greatest darkness just as the brightest light. It takes all its savor from God...for this is all [one's] intention and nothing else has savor for him; and in this he accepts God."[46]

When we attain profound equanimity, God is present to our awareness in every moment and every circumstance—and that is what we want, isn't it? The spiritual journey is simply about knowing God, knowing love, deep within. God dwells within us in equanimity. Then we see God everywhere else as well, undisturbed, like a reflection in a perfectly still pond.

To begin a practice toward equanimity, we can adopt a policy of moderation in everything, beginning with physical things: eat moderately, according to need only; possess moderately; exercise and sleep moderately; work moderately; play moderately. Keep the lid on and the fire down—it will help the emotional pot not to boil over.

When emotions do become immoderate, when we become over-stimulated, excited (happily or unhappily), and tense, pause. P...a...u...s...e. Take a deep breath and look around. Look within. Recall what you really want: God. Even now in the midst of all this upheaval? Especially now, in the midst of all upheavals.

"Seek peace and follow after it" was Saint Benedict's advice to all. Try it. You will find God in it, because "love is the progeny of equanimity."[47]

GOOD HUMOR

When we are even-minded toward all people and all things, when our heart is filled with kindness and trust, when we are learners and not performers, and when we look for the Lord in all people, an unexpected shift often happens: *Life gets humorous.*

Once a woman who lived in nearly constant pain was asked how she could joke so much, for her sense of humor flowed always. She said that in life you can cry a lot or you can laugh a lot, and laughing is better. Did it make her pain less? No, but pain with laughter is better than pain with deadly seriousness.

When we take life with great solemnity, our ego-centricity is very much in control. Only the selfish part of us could think things matter so terribly that we must go around with long faces and sad souls. Well, some people like to point out, the Bible says "Jesus wept," but it never says he laughed. They take that as an indication that we are meant to be very earnest about everything. I think the Bible never tells us Jesus laughed because Jesus' joyousness was so common and obvious to the writers that they didn't think to mention it.

The first time I was on a television show, I was so solemn I looked like wrath itself. What was it? Nervousness about myself and how I would appear to the viewers. I'm not the only person who gets solemn when I'm scared or otherwise contracted. Do you?

When we are open, good humor is everywhere and much of life is downright funny. We won't see it as long as we are so tight about ourselves. As our ego gets put gradually to one side and we focus more and more on the love of the Lord, we relax inwardly and begin to see the humor that God has built into living. We might even start to giggle at the humor in church—and it would be even more beautiful if more people did it.

We can practice by just taking a lighter attitude toward ourselves and everything around us. We don't have to become socially inappropriate, but in our own heart we can stop and correct our perspective every time we find ourselves feeling deadly. Look for the lighter side. Commenting on one of her visions, Julian said, "I understood that we may laugh, to comfort ourselves and rejoice in God."[48]

Best of all, Eckhart speaks again of that joyful inner power in the human being I mentioned before. He says that "there is such delight and such great, immeasurable joy in this power that no one can tell or reveal it all."[49] Joyfulness and lightness are innate in our deepest self, where God dwells.

Two particular practices will intensify our growing awareness of humor and help us be lighter: don't hurry and don't worry.

Hurry, inward haste or outward rushing, is tension-based.

Tension kills humor and stems directly from our ego-centric self. If we slow down enough to relax inside, we will have time to be amused. This does not mean we will accomplish less. It is quite possible to move from here to there efficiently, even quickly, without hurrying. It takes only a few seconds longer than it would take to tear along. (Refusal to hurry is also good for the body—a bonus.)

Hurry will not bring us to God. "God comes more readily if He finds you in leisure," says Angelus.[50]

Worry, too, is anything but an open attitude. Worry is narrow and repetitive. It is a trap. It captures us and holds us tightly in a place where everything seems frighteningly serious and laughing at life becomes impossible. The converse is true, too: it is hard to worry when we are laughing!

If we are practicing contentment and trust, worry will be receding. When we add the practice of good humor, looking for the light side and not wallowing in self-seriousness, our heart will open to the Lord even more freely. We will be able to welcome him into our awareness with good cheer.

Amusement at ourselves is a good practice to promote humility. We ourselves are perhaps the best joke around, when we learn how to see it. When we can laugh at ourselves, and when spouses or friends can laugh at and with one another's peculiarities, love is suddenly present—open-eyed and joyful.

Someone said that angels can fly because they take themselves lightly. Let's imitate them.

PERSEVERANCE AND VIGILANCE

The priests who introduced me to Catholicism used to pray a lot for perseverance. Perseverance is a big-sounding word and it seems a bit ponderous. Its meaning, though, is simple. It means putting one foot in front of the other, then taking another step, then another....Perseverance means: I keep going.

The pace is up to us, the angle of the climb is up to God, but the highest mountain is conquered by putting one foot in front of the other enough times to carry us to the top.

A prayer for perseverance may look far ahead to possible difficulties and temptations. They will come along, no doubt, in the spiritual life as in all of living. Remember, the key to spiritual growth does not lie ahead in the distance. It is here now. It is this particular step, it is this foot being planted ahead of the other right in front of me. We do best to pray to make *this* step firm and to keep moving one foot at a time. "If you wish to arrive, never stop on the way, one must [go] from light to light forever forward."[51]

Perseverance is practiced by doing what we know to do now and by opening to God as we now can, by praying and practicing however we can presently see and presently do. In present practice is joy. In present prayer is peace. In knowing God in *this* step, I am reassured that God will be there in the distance when I get there.

We keep going by stepping along now, by not clinging to what is behind us and by not trying to see further than the next step.

Even that requires watchfulness. So do all our efforts to cooperate with grace, all our moments of receiving grace. Each step inward is a step taken in alertness.

Much happens to us in spiritual growth. Some events feel wonderful, others not so comfortable. Some are strong and challenging, others are gentle and reassuring. All are essentially glorious because all lead to the glory of God. If we are not watchful and alert, we will miss these events. Our next step may be unsteady and we may topple over—though we can always get up and proceed. Still, falling and getting up is much harder than staying alert and stepping vigilantly in the first place.

Inner watchfulness requires effort. All of the attitudes we've been considering will contribute to that effort. For one thing, each of these practices requires some degree of inner watchfulness. They are inner, attitudinal practices, and if we are not watching our inner being, we will not see what the practice entails.

One of the Desert Fathers said, "I think that if a man does not guard his heart well, he will forget and neglect everything he has heard....It is like a lamp filled with oil and lit; if you forget to replenish the oil, gradually it goes out and eventually darkness will prevail."[52]

There is an old story about an inattentive man who sat at the gate of heaven, knowing that it opened at a certain time to let newcomers in. As he waited, he got drowsy and lost his watchfulness. In a few minutes, he heard a clang and looked up to see the gate closing.

It may not be true of heaven after death, but it is true of heaven on earth: if we are not watchful, we will miss our opportunities. Abba Cassian said to his brothers, "Therefore I implore you to...pay attention to yourselves and guard yourselves from the desire to sleep."[53] And sleep means being unaware of God in this very moment.

Watchfulness is a contemplative practice. Learning any form of inner attention is learning to watch, to be alert and aware. It is the core of inward prayer. It can be practiced at any moment whatsoever.

Whenever we remember to be watchful, we turn our attention to our inner being, where the Lord waits for us. We can be doing anything else at the time if the power of our alertness is strong enough. For that power, we practice. Every single time we feel an inner tug, every time something reminds us, every time we remember God spontaneously, we watch what is occurring within. We need not become involved in it or get carried away by it. We only watch it.

The practice of such watchfulness will gradually enable us to relate differently to all aspects of ourselves, including our emotions and our thoughts. Watching them is quite different from identifying with them or collapsing into them. Watch! If not in this moment then in the next, you will surely find the Lord. We want to "make ourselves ready for his call, keeping awake by the doors of our dwellings, whenever He should come and knock."[54]

APPRECIATION OF SILENCE

Most Westerners in the late twentieth century do not seek solitude much, nor do we value silence. We enter our houses and go straight to the TV or stereo. On with the sound and pictures! The thought of being totally silent even for an eight-day retreat is appalling to most people.

Although God may be perceived in people, in events, in music, and in all beauty, God is most fully known in profound silence. It need not necessarily be in quiet circumstances, although physical silence is certainly helpful in the beginning. Essentially, this profound silence is interior. The silence of our inner self is a piece, as it were, of the vast loving silence of God.

You may have had an experience like the following. We were driving across a vast stretch of desert one spring afternoon. We approached an especially interesting formation of rocks and flowers, so we stopped the car and turned off the engine. Silence. No sound. Not the slightest whisper. We got out of the car; the doors closing were thunder. Again, the vast soundlessness. Stillness almost palpable. Something deep inside me sighed, let go, opened to the silence. It was not empty, this serenity, but dynamic and full. It said, "God."

For nearly two thousand years, the value of silence as a means of finding God has been attested to by people who sought it in monasteries or hermitages or other separate ways of life. But even in those places, responsibilities and other people were a part of their life. The silence of the physical desert may help, but unless the inner being knows silence, God is still hard to experience.

In reality, silence does not interrupt sound. Sound interrupts silence. Silence lives deep within our own being, and this inner silence is where we meet the Lord of love. This inner silence is perpetual. It lives always beneath every outer sound. When you have heard it within, you can hear it under even the worst racket, because it is interior to everything.

Inner watchfulness will take us to silence. Here is an exercise to help us appreciate silence—and we have to do this alone (or with other silent people). Find a quiet, comfortable place. Close your eyes. Notice (do not change) your breathing. There is a pause at the end of each exhale. Focus your watchful attention on that pause. It is silent. No air is moving there, no thoughts either. In that pause is silence. In that pause between breaths—it happens thousands of times a day—is God. Watch for him there.

"The voice of God is heard: Listen within and seek; Were you but always silent, he'd never cease to speak," Angelus tells us.[55] Find God in interior stillness only once and your attitude toward silence and solitude will be changed. Find God in that silence a hundred times and silence will be your great love, solitude your dear friend, because there you come face to face with the Lord your heart seeks.

LOVE

If you have been pondering these attitudes as you read, you have noticed that every one of them leads to love. Love, of course, is more than an attitude; it is God, infinite and beckoning and inviting, filling and comforting and challenging. Learning to love is learning to be like God so as to eventually be one with him.

In the *Cloud* we read that in the interior spiritual work, "God is loved above every creature purely and simply for his own sake. Indeed the very heart of this work is nothing else but a naked intent toward God for his own sake."[56]

Love is the attitude, the practice, the way, and the goal. Love is God. When we are drenched in love, we will be deified by God's loving grace. We will be home in God. We will be love.

In our efforts to cultivate high attitudes and practice the virtues, we take the advice of Abba Poemen: "When a man prepares to build a house, he gathers together all he needs to be able to construct it, and he collects different sorts of materials. So it is with us; let us acquire a little of all the virtues."[57]

And we remember with Angelus Silesius that "God is each virtue's goal, its impulse and its crown."[58]

Notes

[1] *Angelus,* p. 54.

[2] *Maximus,* p. 197.

[3] Gregory, p. 101.

[4] Gregory, p. 82.

[5] *Maximus,* p. 182.

[6] Gregory, p. 226.

[7] *Angelus,* p. 113.

[8] *Cloud,* p. 47.

[9] *Bernard,* p. 215.

[10] *Symeon,* p. 171.

[11] Gregory, p. 154.

[12] *Catherine,* p. 113.

[13] *Eckhart,* Colledge and McGinn, p. 215.

[14] *Birgitta,* p. 105.

[15] *Angelus,* p. 76.

[16] Gregory, p. 148.

[17] *Birgitta,* p. 84.

[18] *Eckhart,* Colledge and McGinn, p. 263.

[19] *Birgitta,* p. 93.

[20] *Symeon,* pp. 87-88.

[21] *Eckhart,* Colledge and McGinn, p. 207.

[22] *Bernard,* p. 226.

[23] Matthew Fox, *Illuminations of Hildegard of Bingen* (Sante Fe, NM: Bear and Co., 1985), p. 40.

[24] *Hildegard,* pp. 40-41.

[25] *Hildegard's Scivias,* ed. Bruce Hozeski (Sante Fe, NM: Bear and Co., 1986), p. 68.

[26] *Hildegard,* p. 75.

[27] *Evagrius,* p. 75.

[28] *Julian,* p. 218.

[29] *Julian,* p. 217.

[30] *Julian,* p. 216.

[31] *Bernard,* p. 103.

[32] *Eckhart,* Colledge and McGinn, p. 217.

[33] *Catherine,* p. 301.

[34] *Catherine,* p. 168.

[35] *Symeon,* p. 292.

[36] *Cloud,* p. 68.

37 Gregory, p. 163.
38 *Evagrius*, p. 75.
39 *Eckhart*, Colledge and McGinn, p. 192.
40 *Sayings*, p. 113.
41 Yushi Nomura, *Desert Wisdom* (Garden City, NY: Doubleday, 1982), p. 117.
42 *Bernard*, p. 112.
43 *Sayings*, p. 113.
44 *Angelus*, p. 66.
45 *Evagrius*, p. 34.
46 Eckhart, Colledge and McGinn, pp. 260-261.
47 *Evagrius*, p. 36 (translation of "agape is the progeny of apatheia").
48 *Julian*, p. 217.
49 *Eckhart*, Colledge and McGinn, p. 180.
50 *Angelus*, p. 115.
51 *Angelus*, p. 81.
52 *Sayings*, p. 136.
53 *Sayings*, p. 98.
54 Gregory, p. 245.
55 *Angelus*, p. 124.
56 *Cloud*, p. 80.
57 *Sayings*, p. 156.
58 *Angelus*, p. 88.

Circumstances
of Daily Life

Every human life includes relationships with other people, work to do, decisions to make, circumstances to experience, money to earn and use, recreation to enjoy. For a life with a spiritual purpose, there are also church life and personal spiritual practices. Every bit of our living can be approached as a spiritual practice, that is, with a spiritual goal. Spiritual life will ultimately embrace all aspects of our day-to-day living. Just as we ourselves participate in them all, so our spirituality will eventually pervade them all. Everything will be transformed in God by the gracious action of the Spirit—and by our cooperation with divine grace. Our cooperation is grounded in our attitude of practicing in every moment.

When I was young, I felt quite alone in my efforts to "do the right thing." So I could never understand why people like Zechariah (John the Baptist's father) and Moses and Jeremiah argued with God's messengers—an angel, a burning bush, a voice. What wouldn't I have given for similar "sky-writing" to tell me what to do! I was years in learning what was amiss with this wish, but gradually I did begin to see how God guided me.

God's guidance came mostly through the circumstances of my daily life, punctuated by big events. Now, after years of asking other people how their guidance comes to them, I find that I'm in the majority. All of us have times of insight, intuition, and maybe even inner words or pictures. Most of us most of the time, however, are taught by circumstances.

With a serious yes to God's invitation, one's circumstances change. Different events occur in our lives than would have happened otherwise. In the beginning, every day may still look like every day. But after a while, we see that those "every days" are leading us in a Godward direction if we are cooperating with God's constant, gracious love. We aim to cooperate so that every moment of all our activities is open to God's loving penetration.

Here's a first step in cooperating with grace in all our daily circumstances: *Look within, toward God.* Doing this allows God into all our circumstances and activities. Everything we do then becomes a lovely practice-toward-God.

Sometimes we need to take time away from our activities in order to look within. Often we only need to remember our purpose and shift our attention from the external events to the interior of our being. This shift is possible in the midst of any activity. At first, we may forget to do it more often than we remember. It may be a long while before our inward attention is stable. After all, we are heavily conditioned to focus outward and have little practice focusing inwardly. Yet nothing intrinsic to any circumstance itself makes the shift impossible.

Our inner attention itself is prayer, because the Lord is within.

If we are cultivating new attitudes, as suggested in "Attitudes to Be Cultivated" (page 69), we quickly find that any event, any situation, is an opportunity to practice. Each situation will call for one or another of those new attitudes we wish to cultivate. Thus, no matter what happens in our lives, we can proceed toward God. We look within, we attend, we ask God what is given and what is needed, both in the situation and in our response to it. Then we set ourselves to practice before the Lord. Of every situation we can silently say, "This, too, is practice; thank you, Lord, for this opportunity."

A particular step we can always take is to offer the situation, our practice, and the results to our loving Lord. It is especially valuable to release the results from our concern. Abba Nilus said, "Do not be always wanting everything to turn out as you think it should, but rather as God pleases, then you will be undisturbed and thankful in your prayer."[1]

Our detachment grows with this effort and likewise our love for God, who gives the results. God alone knows how everything can work for our best, our highest. Loving God, we want God's will to come out of every situation. So we do our work, and we let God determine the outcome.

The more we look within, find the gift and the practice, then obey the guidance, the more we see God's love involved in every event in our everyday life. The more we find God, the more closely we look into every event, asking in our heart, "Lord, what have you in this for me to receive or to practice?" We are treasure-troving in our own life.

Usually, we experience circumstances immediately as pleasant or unpleasant—and they can be pleasant in the extreme or unpleasant in the extreme. We may hope they will never end or wish they had never begun. Neither of these perfectly natural responses is helpful to spiritual life.

To move beyond this automatic response, try these practices:

First, instead of dwelling on whether you like this particular situation or not, ask yourself, "What is really going on here?" Let yourself see the situation as clearly and objectively as possible. This does not mean without emotion. Emotion plays a part, but it is never the whole. It is quite possible to become aware of all aspects of our responses. Practice seeing all parts of a situation, inner and outer, and how they all are working together, while asking for God's grace to help you perceive the gift in the whole.

Second, give thanks—even if it is a stretch for your faith—for this particular gift in these circumstances. Abba Benjamin's last words to his disciples were, "Be joyful at all times, pray without ceasing, and give thanks for all things."[2] Thanksgiving may not be easy, especially if major changes occur or if pain is involved. Gratitude for the gift does not mean you have to like the situation. God's gifts sometimes are drawn out of terrible circumstances. We can trust that God will not damage our innermost being nor allow situations to do that.

The best way to open yourself to the Spirit's action in every situation is by gratitude.

In time, as we go through experiences with awareness and as we grow in them, we begin to see that truly "all things work for good for those who love God" (Romans 8:28). When we recognize this, we can be contented and trustful no matter what is happening.

Throughout both pleasant and unpleasant circumstances, we remember that nothing stays the same, especially not our emotions. Wonderful situations come and go, just as unwelcome situations come and go. About the only event that is permanent is the death of a loved one. That relationship will no longer be there in the same way as before. Yet even in bereavement, the quality of our experience changes with time, and God still gives wonderful gifts to those who love him.

Knowing that nothing remains the same, we are invited to give ourselves generously to whatever life brings for as long as it lasts. We choose not to hold ourselves back from experience in self-protective ways but to devote our energies willingly to the path immediately at our feet. If you are given a trip to Europe (as happened to my husband and me), then go and savor every moment. If illness comes, take the opportunity to heal at a new level; don't just avoid pain but take up the effort to be wholly well. If a task looks overwhelming, plunge in, trusting and offering every step to God. If you get to play awhile, play with delight and verve. By doing everything totally and offering it to God, you will open your heart to him. Your awareness of the Spirit within will intensify.

The pleasant circumstance will carry us to God lightly, on wings of enjoyment and thankfulness, provided that we do not cling to it but allow it to please us and go, leaving its gifts. The unpleasant circumstance can carry us to God as well, in the quiet of a heart stilled by acceptance of pain. For God gives gifts in the wake of pain also.

Let us welcome all the opportunities as God sends them and accept the gifts he offers. Then we will come little by little to live constantly in the love that is God.

So if you have said yes to God, you may expect circumstances to guide your next step, to provide your task and your gift straight from the Lord to your own innermost being.

Now let's think about several areas of our daily life and reflect a little about how to experience God in each of them. The following comments are meant to stimulate your own thinking. They are suggestive. Only you can complete them by working with them in your own circumstances.

DECISION-MAKING

Often we can mold circumstances by our own decisions. In our circumstances, we receive not only the gifts of God but also the lawful consequences. God brings us closer to himself through both gift and consequence.

We've just considered life's events as pleasant or unpleasant. From a spiritual perspective, these categories are incomplete: the pleasant (easily identified) are not always beneficial, and the unpleasant (likewise easily identified) are not always harmful.

As Hildegard of Bingen writes, "The soul investigates things in the same way that wheat is separated from the chaff. It inquires whether things are useful or useless, or lovable or hateful, or whether they relate to life or to death."[3] Exactly. So our task, as we learn to cooperate with God, is to discern when a situation or action is beneficial to our spiritual growth and when one is harmful to it—then to live accordingly.

Our decisions will be made at two levels. First, can we or do we wish to change the circumstances? This is a question of externals. Second, what shall our response be? This is an inner decision. The externals are not always available to our control. The inner decision always is.

So we ask, "Will this option I'm considering help me to come closer to God or not?" In spiritual life, we do not stand still but always move either toward God or away from God. So if something does not help us move toward God, it is a hindrance.

Something that does not take us toward God may not be, in itself, at all evil. A merchant, for example, may find that too much success is fine in itself. Yet this merchant may wish to limit her work so as to have time and energy for more interior efforts.

Each time a decision has to be made, it is helpful to avoid stereotypes of what is good, approaching each situation afresh. For example, someone may have to decide between working for the homeless and contributing that same time and energy to one's own home and family. This person may assume that working for the homeless is better, but it may not be better for that particular person's relationship with God. Or vice versa.

The foreseeable benefits for our relationship to God are the determining factors in any and all decisions. Since closer knowledge of God is our all-embracing aim, all decisions can be made with the intention that they serve our love of God.

What we cannot do in our relationship with God, God is responsible for. Let us never forget that God can do what he wishes and that he always sees more options than we do. In the spiritual journey, it is our task to do what the Lord gives us. He will keep us plenty busy! The rest is God's responsibility.

TAKE CARE OF YOURSELF

You are God's precious creation, made in God's Image. Your body is the vehicle for the Spirit of God, and "you are not your own" (1 Corinthians 6:19). You are God's. If you love God and wish to serve him, then how do you take care of what is precious to him? Bernard of Clairvaux says that the highest kind of love is that which a person has for himself or herself for the sake of God.

Some of us have the idea that taking good care of ourselves is selfish, that we should give all our time and energies to other people. This is an error. If we try to live that way, we end up weakened and often ill. That is not God's way. Nor should we neglect ourselves from a mistaken notion of self-denial or asceticism.

Taking care of ourselves is a privilege and a duty. It is a privilege because in caring for ourselves, we are caring for part of God's creation; we are serving God. It is a duty because if we neglect ourselves, we are actually despising God's will for us.

Taking care of ourselves means caring for the body, neither treating it badly nor indulging its every whim. Maximus urges that we give the body what is "necessary for life. In this way one loves it without passion and rears it as an associate in divine things and takes care of it only with those things which satisfy its needs."[4] That means doing what we know to do for good health and learning about nutrition and exercise. It means moderation in all physical things. It means keeping the body clean and well-groomed. As we stated in "General Principles of Spiritual Life" (page 27), the body is an integral part of our spiritual life. It should be kept as strong and healthy as possible.

Taking care of our mind and emotions means not taking them too seriously nor overidentifying with them. We can train them, heal them as needed, and give them their due—but no more than that. We do not necessarily believe everything they tell us. We observe them and respect them as creations of God, but we order our life around our higher aim: our loving desire for oneness with God.

Because God made us, self-care is spiritual practice. So when I exercise, I offer it to the Lord, and when I wash or dress or eat, I do the same. If I cannot offer something to God honestly, then I need to examine whether I really want to do it or whether God wants me to do it.

In periods of stress, such as illness or the death of a loved one, we are tempted to neglect ourselves. Yet we need to take gentle care of ourselves especially in such times because they are often times of weakened purpose. Our own debilitation can only worsen the whole situation. If we strengthen ourselves by self-care and offer it to God, then difficulties and pains will trouble us less. We will be able to rest in God's gifts more easily and fully if we are well cared for—by our own selves.

OUR RELATIONSHIPS:
MARRIAGE, FAMILY, FRIENDS

In our relationships with other people, we receive many of our loveliest gifts from God. Our relationships also teach us some of our most essential lessons in living for God. We need relationships with others from our birth until our death. We want them. We seek them. We want to receive from other people, and we also want to give. Most profoundly, we long to relate to others in mutual love.

If we are cultivating the attitude of seeing God in other people, no better field practice exists than our relationships with family and friends. Of course, our practice will not be confined to those close circles, but we can well begin there. If we see God in our spouse, our children, our relatives, and our friends, our relationships with these people will be more loving and more intimate, just as we desire them to be. The relationships will become wonderful experiences as well as good training ground.

For spiritual growth, we ask ourselves one major question about each relationship: What qualities do I want to *put into* this relationship? Then we pray about it, asking how to love God in the relationship, how to serve God in it, how to be and how to grow within the relationship so that closeness to God is fostered.

The answers to these questions will vary with every individual and every relationship. The principles involved are common to all relationships, differing only in their intensity and intimacy and in the forms of expression peculiar to each one. Spousal relationships are not lived in the same form as friendships, for example, but love lives in both.

Love in a relationship includes respect for all people involved, be it two or twenty. Love implies that no one is violated and no one habitually capitulates to another. Some Christians (especially women,

I think) may assume that to love another means to give that one everything he or she wants at whatever cost to ourselves. Capitulation is not love, any more than domination is love. God's love for us all seeks the best for *each* person in the relationship.

The saints were strong people, not the least bit wimpy. They submitted to God and to God's will. They were not blown about by other people's opinions or threats. The life of every saint is a study in how to live in charity for all but capitulation to none except God. In that way, the highest interests of all people are served. That is the aim of love.

In any event within a relationship, we may seek God and God's will for everyone involved. When we remember to look within for God's gift and the practice inherent in the situation, we can see more clearly what is happening. This holds true even in an argument. If we can see the argument as practice in love instead of as a battle to come out ahead of the other person, we will be less intent on getting in the winning word and more intent on communication and shared life. These lead to lively loving—and to God.

If we offer our best to God in others, then the results will be the Lord's. Practicing in this way is seldom easy because our egos are so involved. But then *ease* is not the point. The point is to create closer and more loving relationships with others and with God. Specific actions and choices will be unique to each person, each relationship.

If we live in a family, then family life is our responsibility before God and our spiritual opportunity. To the extent that we give ourselves to God through family life and service to family members, God will meet us there. Then our family duty itself becomes our spiritual pathway to the Lord and a profound spiritual practice. As always, our attitudes and the purpose we seek in family life will determine its quality. If we want to serve God through family and friendship, we can.

All relationships are fields for the practice of loving-kindess and other vital attitudes. Sometimes one's spiritual life grows more through loving presence to a family member than by participation in a church event or community project. Sometimes the opposite will be closer to God's will. Each decision must be made in the light of God's immediate guidance. In the deciding, we'll recall what we already have learned of spiritual principles.

Does all this sound a little like walking a tightrope? Yes, sometimes relationships and related decisions can challenge our clearest sight and our strongest resolve. But they are lovely in themselves, too. They become a beautiful, unending adventure when we look inside, find our balance, then practice right on the spot. In so doing, the lover of God loves God more because God, who is love, is increasing in the heart.

OUR SEXUALITY

Because so many traditional models of Christian spirituality are celibate and because our own society has so confused us about sexuality, we might question whether our sexual life can serve our spiritual life. It can.

The principles of life toward God that affect our sexual activity are these: Sex is good and God intended us to enjoy it; sex belongs to marriage; it may be offered to God; we can include God in it; moderation applies here as everywhere.

God intended humans to enjoy sexual intimacy, just as he intended us to have children. Both aspects are intricately bound up in our sexual expression, and neither is bad. For those vowed to celibacy, the pleasure in sex is a temptation. For persons vowed to another in marriage, the pleasure in sex is a blessing and an exquisite expression of their mutual love. The spiritual value or disvalue of sex, like many other values in life, lies not in sex itself but in our attitude toward it and the purposes for which we use it.

Of course, sex is misused both inside and outside of marriage. Misuse is rooted in a twisted attitude of the heart, as when sex is a selfish activity without regard for the partner. Human sexual potential itself, including both its pleasures and the bearing of children, is good and can support spiritual effort.

In the spiritual use of all pleasures, two principles apply: moderation and gratitude. God means for us to enjoy our pleasures—they are divine gifts. He does not mean for us to be addicted to them, to use them selfishly, or to cling to them at the expense of relationship with himself. We can revel in our pleasures—sexual pleasure included—and let them go past, giving hearty thanks to the Lord for the lovely gift.

Pleasures are to be enjoyed in moderation. If we bury our lives in pleasure-seeking and make all our decisions based on the possibility of pleasurable outcome, we will not grow closer to God because the focus is on ourselves rather than on God. Sexual pleasure is a splendid, powerful drive that we can enjoy in moderation. Only then can we look within and use it for practice.

For the deep lover of God, sexual expression is subordinate to spiritual possibility, as is everything else in life. The more we practice putting God first, the sooner sex will take its rightful place. What we put second to God is not bad; it is merely second. Make God the priority and stay in balance—simple to say, not always easy to do.

Prayer and sex? Prayer *in* sex? Why not? If spouses are agreed on a commitment to a life of prayer and to including their sexual experience in it, they may pray—out loud and together or silently in the heart—before, during, and after sexual intercourse. If they are not agreed, the one who longs for God may pray in the heart. We may offer the whole of lovemaking to God, who invented it. We may find God present in making love to the partner God has given us. God is not excluded from our sexuality.

By including our sexuality in our relationship with God, we both sanctify sex, as was intended for married people, and are drawn yet another step toward living totally for God.

If we are single, genital expression of sexuality probably will confuse our spiritual intentions. Single folks can learn to use those very energies to enhance spiritual practice, particularly inward prayer. Great inner power is to be found in this use of sexual energies. One reason several religious traditions, including Christianity, value celibacy is that it can powerfully enhance contemplative prayer.

Whether we are single by circumstance or by vow, this opportunity is open to us.

Married or single, our sexual energies—like our whole being—were created by God, are loved by God, and are intrinsically good. Let's stop disparaging sexuality on the one hand and behaving as if it were all-determining on the other. Let's take it as it was meant to be—a good gift of God, life-giving when used well. Sex is just one among many aspects of life that can promote spirituality or detract from it, depending on our attitude toward it and the use we make of it.

OUR HOME

My husband, John, says, "The home is a sacred place, so all the tasks we do there are sacred acts." He probably said it first when I was complaining about housework—or being amazed at his willingness to do it. So I learned from him about how one's dwelling can support spiritual life if we treat it like the dwelling of God, a temple, a sacred space.

Looking within, I find that I often take housework quite for granted; there are so many more interesting things to do. So, seeing my attitude, I can practice toward God by adopting John's view and caring for our house with more attention and more generosity. I can also develop more appreciation for our home by giving thanks for it just as it is, no matter what luxuries may be missing.

Since I do, in fact, use our home as a temple for worship and prayer, I try to remember to offer to God every bit of work and play that takes place there. Most of the tasks we do in a home are relatively mindless. That fact is a great opportunity; we can turn our attention inward more easily and pray or sing to God, offering our heart and mind to the Lord while our bodies are busy with vacuum or dishcloth.

We can also practice awareness by giving close attention to everything we do in the house, from noticing where we put our glasses or shoes to really seeing the miracle of our hands at work or noticing the exact qualities in making a cup of coffee. Any effort to stay attentive during ordinary activity is a challenge. Its purpose is to train the mind so that it can be receptive to the Lord. Attentiveness draws us again into the present moment where God can be found.

Our environment affects our mind—another reason to treat our home as sacred space. Our living space helps us most when it is clean, relatively clutter-free, and as beautiful as we can make it. Prayer comes most easily in a lovely setting, one of the reasons churches are intended to be beautiful. Moreover, if we are seeking God in our whole selves, our home can support us best when it is lovely and comfortable.

Who would want to worship God in a cluttered or dirty church? How can we offer our home to God if it is a mess?

OUR WORK

Every human being must work. It is built into our nature. We work at home, of course, but most of us must also work to earn a living. All work contributes to someone's welfare. The work itself may be beneficial to the world, or the resulting paycheck may enable a family to live. Even the desert hermits worked, often braiding reeds for baskets. They worked in order to eat but for a deeper purpose as well. "As far as you can, do some manual work so as to be able to give alms," advised Abba Poemen.[5] These ascetics who owned almost nothing chose to work in order to give!

If work is to support spiritual life, we can use it as practice, too, looking within for its gifts and lessons and offering it to God. In working, as in everything else, our primary purpose is to draw near to God, so it is to be submitted to God. "Everything you do as a commandment of God is the work of the soul; but to work...for a personal motive ought to be held as subordinate" is Abba Theodore's advice.[6]

Three questions can help us discern how our work supports our spiritual life or how we may turn it to that purpose. First, is our work constructive? If the intrinsic purpose of the job is to destroy, it is highly doubtful that it would support spiritual effort.

I have known people in prison who considered thievery their profession. They had a certain ethic about their "work," and they didn't steal from neighbors or people they respected. They gave it great attention and learned their skills well. But this "profession" would hardly support spiritual aims. The case is not always so clear, however. Each worker will examine his or her own job to see if it actually does contribute constructively to the world.

Second, what quality do we put into our work? If we are offering the work to God, then we want to give it our very best. We want to do it with love. We are preparing a gift for the One our heart seeks. How could we think of being lazy or doing slipshod work? Working as an offering to God holds us close to him.

Third, how do we handle relationships in the workplace?

As with our other relationships, we must look for God in our coworkers. We look within, seek God's gift and our practice, and behave accordingly. We seek to cooperate with coworkers, helping instead of competing against them. We practice loving-kindness and forgiveness. We offer our work relationships to God.

Since our work fills a major portion of our time and energy, it is vital to use the workplace as a field of spiritual practice. Otherwise, we compartmentalize our lives and our selves and keep God out. People have devised many reminders for themselves, including taking prayer breaks instead of coffee breaks or taking a few minutes to stretch the body and the spirit in every hour or so of work. It is a matter of practicality. Experiment a bit, then stick with the practice that brings you closer to God in love and in awareness of his presence.

OUR MONEY

We might like to think that money is neutral when it comes to God, but it is not. Money is, after all, only an extension of our own energies in a different form. We work to get it, and we decide how to spend it. How can we look within, find a practice, and offer our money to God?

We first take a look at our attitude about money. Are we grabby? Untrusting or anxious? Which of the attitudes we practice cultivating could be applied to our money? How attached are we to money and dreams of money?

Maximus says, "There are three reasons for the love of money: pleasure-seeking, vainglory, and lack of faith. The hedonist loves money because with it he lives in luxury; the vain person because with it he can be praised; the person who lacks faith because he can hide it and keep it while in fear of hunger, or old age, or illness, or exile. He lays his hope on it rather than on God the maker and provider of the whole creation."[7]

Our society's valuation of money is further distorted. We have made it extremely private, as if it really tells everything about us. We will talk with others about every other detail of our lives—bathroom and bedroom included—but not about how much money we make or how much we paid for our possessions. This intensity about money indicates that we identify ourselves—our worth as persons, our privacy, and our happiness—altogether too closely with our money. Our attachment to it is subtle and pervasive, like a spiderweb all over our lives. So strong an attachment does not support a deep desire for God.

On the other hand, we often seem to assume that money is the one thing God cannot control, that we have to (and often want to) control our money totally ourselves. That is an error. God controls money just as totally as he does everything else, and when we have said yes to God, the quality of our feelings about money will change. The presence and meaning of money in our lives will also change, and no one can predict just how long that will take.

With all this attachment going on in us, one of the best things we can do with money to deepen our relationship with God is give it away. Tithing is a wonderful practice and saves us making endless decisions. Tithing means that we determine a percentage of our income "off the top," then—give it away! Choose a charity, or several, give it to the church or to local needs—it matters little which good cause you choose. In giving our money, we give a bit of ourselves and our efforts.

And while you're signing the checks, rejoice and give thanks that you are able to help the world!

Giving decreases our own tendency to cling to what we imagine to be security. The only lasting security is in God. In bidding us not to worry about what we are to eat or drink, Jesus promised that if we "seek first the kingdom [of God] and his righteousness...all these things will be given you besides" (Matthew 6:33). Let us not imagine that our security lies in money.

Once a man said to me, "I'm too poor to give anything away." Nonsense. Mahatma Gandhi asked his poverty-stricken followers to save three grains of rice from each meal until they had a bowlful, then to give it away. The amount is not important. The giving is.

Avoiding worry about money and arguments about it (especially with spouses) are two other good practices. Another excellent practice is to cultivate the attitude that the money is put into our accounts by the Lord, to spend for him. We then are agents of the Lord. What is the inner effect of this change in viewpoint? Try it; you may be surprised at the personal power suddenly available to you. You may be even more surprised about the effect such a change will bring to your relationship with God.

Such practices help put money in its proper place, as a fact of life that also belongs on our journey to God. Do we use money to cooperate with grace? Or does our attitude toward money hinder our growth toward the God of our hearts?

RECREATION
AND LEISURE TIME

If we think that life toward God is all solemn and serious and that we have to work at it without variation, we are simply mistaken. Life toward God, living in love and increasing joy, includes enjoying our leisure and recreation to their fullest.

Life is not meant to be a drudgery, and especially not spiritual life. It is meant to be a celebration of love because God is in it. If we habitually miss out on the party, we need once again to look within and find out what attitudes prevent us from enjoyment.

Almost any activity can be playful. One person may play at hikes that another person finds the most awful effort. Another person may prefer movies, while someone else may dance under the moon. What we do does not matter as much as the zest and fun we find in it.

Play time is also practice time, time to plunge more deeply into love of God by the sheer delight of our enjoyments. Who gives us our pleasures? Our heart can overflow with gratitude for these experiences and bring us to rejoice directly in the Giver. We play, then, not in isolation nor only with our family and friends but with God present in our leisure activities.

Even Evagrius, living an ascetic life in the desert, knew this. "Understand this point well: one is to worship him even in spiritual relaxations and in times of good cheer with even more piety and reverence."[8]

One caution may be in order. Some of us think we should do all the things others think are fun. Here, too, love and seeking mutual options can be important. I may choose to go with my husband to a baseball game, which I find boring in itself. But I can make it fun if I'm willing to look and to be playful at heart. Even fun is in the attitude we take. We do not have to participate in sports or games to be playful in our activities—it is our attitude that counts. If we don't know how to enjoy the things of earth, how can we enjoy God?

We may also inspect our attitude about leisure-time activities. If we use them merely for diversion, for a time of nonattention to ourselves or to God, they won't support our spiritual life. Growing toward God includes the ability to increase our focus, and simply throwing away our energy does not help. When we choose recreation, then, we choose something that genuinely nourishes us, refreshes us, and does not take us so far away from inner awareness that it is an effort to return. This is the key principle for bringing our play into our relationship with God.

Since many of us spend leisure time with publications and television, it is worth noting that our relation to the media often needs examination and conscious decision. Does our use of newspapers, magazines, and television support our spiritual life or not? This is not a question of "what can it hurt?" but rather a look at the more positive side—does it help? When does it help? Do we desire God enough to use even television, magazines, and newspapers only as they support our inner journey?

In our recreation, as in all areas of our life, we offer our participation to God. He is there anyway. Do we imagine that when we step cnto a sailboat, God stays ashore? Or that when we enter a movie, God waits on the sidewalk? Or that when we're in the heat of a tennis match, God is waiting in the church pew? We play, it is lovely, and we can revel in God in the midst of our play. Let's not neglect this special joy.

PARTICULAR SPIRITUAL PRACTICES

For one who longs for God, every day will include some form of deliberate spiritual practice. Of course, our efforts continue to cooperate with God in all aspects of our activities. Yet we need to set aside some special time each day to *be* in relationship to God, either directly in deep prayer or through a mediator such as Scripture. It has been said a million times, but it remains true: lovers who never spend time alone together do not remain in love. So it is with God, also.

Some people may object, "But God is present all the time in my heart. Why do I have to take special time out for him?" Of course, God is present. But are *you* present all the time? It takes years of practice to be present to God in every moment, every activity. That's our goal! Furthermore, no one *has* to take time for God. But the lover of God needs it, wants it.

There are almost as many spiritual practices or disciplines as there are people, and each person will look for those that are most effective for him or her. Many books deal with daily disciplines. Here are three disciplines I believe to be essential.

Prayer

Prayer is *the* absolutely essential daily practice. How can we be close to God unless we spend time with him? In "Attitudes to Be Cultivated" (page 69), Scripture reading and prayer were mentioned as aids for deepening our loving desire of God. They do that, and they also become our relationship with God. We experience prayer and Scripture as both means and end.

Prayer takes many forms, and individuals pray according to their need and their awareness of possibilities. God also guides the longing heart into forms of prayer that may not have been known beforehand. We petition God for our desires, for our loved ones, and for their needs. We praise God for his truth, beauty, and love. We thank God for all the blessings in our lives. We may visualize the Scriptures—a form of prayer as old as Christianity. We may pray in our own words or the words of a specially loved prayer, such as the rosary. All forms of prayer are good, and most of them will be practiced at some time by everyone.

Of all the forms of prayer, the most powerful is contemplative prayer, also called centering prayer or Christian meditation. (*Meditation* traditionally often means "reflective thinking," but most frequently today it refers to contemplative, or centering, prayer.) Contemplative prayer is accessible to everyone, though—like everything else—it will be easier for some people than for others. It is not a "special calling" reserved for a few. God invites all who desire intimacy with him to this form of prayer. It does require persistent practice, however.

The *Cloud* describes contemplative prayer for us. "This is what you are to do: lift your heart up to the Lord, with a gentle stirring of love desiring him for his own sake and not for his gifts. Center all your attention and desire on him and let this be the sole concern of your mind and heart. Do all in your power to forget everything else, keeping your thoughts and desires free from involvement with any of God's creatures...It is this which gives God the greatest delight."[9]

The practice of contemplative prayer is simplicity itself (which does not mean we will find it easy). Here are the basics:

♦ Sit comfortably, spine straight.
♦ Quiet down inside.
♦ Turn your attention lovingly to the Lord.
♦ Sit still. Be open.
♦ Wait upon the Lord.

Because we are so seldom inwardly quiet and because steady attention is a high and rather rare capacity, we can help ourselves in several commonly used ways. The most frequent of these is a prayer-word or phrase (Father John Main, O.S.B., calls this word or phrase by its Indian name *mantra*).

The prayer-word is just that: a word or phrase meaningful to the pray-er that is repeated to help keep the mind quiet and the attention focused. It may be repeated rhythmically with the breath or used to recall the mind when it has wandered. Each person may need to experiment awhile to find the most helpful practice, then stick with it.

The *Cloud* advises that "if you want to gather all your desire into one simple word that the mind can easily retain, choose a short word rather than a long one. A one-syllable word such as 'God' or 'love' is best. But choose one that is meaningful to you. Then fix it in your mind so that it will remain there come what may."[10]

Particular postures are sometimes helpful for focus, but one consistent guideline is suggested: be at ease and keep the spine straight. The reason for a straight spine is that the body is designed to be firmly supported on it, and the body will eventually begin to squirm and distract you if the spine is not straight.

Another helpful point is timing. It is best to pray daily and at the same time each day if possible. It is easiest on an empty stomach, when one is fully awake. Many find the first thing in the morning is the best time.

How long should you pray this way? Advice ranges from twenty minutes to an hour or however the Lord leads you. To begin, twenty minutes is a fine minimum. Meditating twice daily is good, too. You may set a timer if you wish. If you do, put it in another room or use one with a soft sound. In deep meditative silence, a sudden sound can jangle the system.

In the beginning, contemplative prayer is a practice, because twentieth-century Westerners are unaccustomed to silence. As we learn the mechanics, we find that this time in silent solitude with God is the core, the essence, the actuality, of our relationship with God. Everything else we do in our daily life will either support this prayer or it won't. In this prayer, however, we find our deepest mutual touch with the Lord. All the mystics, no matter where they began, eventually were drawn into this form of prayer. The experience of God in contemplative prayer is the foundation. It is in this prayer that God will give us everything, even himself.

Spiritual Reading

Spiritual reading can be of Scripture or other writings about spiritual life or about God. Reading is food for the mind, and the mind can be a best friend on this journey inward. It is vital that our understanding—of our journey, of our faith, and of our goal—be sound and reliable.

Our minds are powerful. The mind needs to be saturated with helpful ideas, uplifting thoughts, encouraging instruction and clear warnings against danger spots. The more our thinking is God-centered, the more the rest of our living will turn to God as well. Reading is an excellent tool to turn our habitual thoughts toward God. The *Cloud* agrees: "Beginners and those a little advanced who do not make the effort to ponder God's word should not be surprised if they are unable to pray. Experience bears this out."[11]

Notice that the writer says "ponder." The purpose of spiritual reading is not only to "finish the book." And it certainly is not to pass an exam. Spiritual reading aims to let truth and beauty sink deep into us. To that end, we want to read reflectively, slowly, pausing to think about and pray over whatever strikes us as interesting or puzzling. It is good to jot notes in the margins, to be in conversation with the writer. Yes, write in your Bible. If you don't own a Bible you want to write in, buy one for that purpose. (Editions printed on sturdy paper and with wide margins are available.)

Then think about what you have read. Ask yourself questions like these: What does this seem to mean for me? What is its meaning about my external life—activities, relationships, work, and so forth? What is its meaning for my inner life? Is it analogous to my interior experience or need? What insights are here about the Lord and how the Spirit works with me? How can I apply this insight to my daily efforts? What if this were said by God directly to me?

The *Cloud* advises that "God's word, written or spoken, is like a mirror....When a person discovers in a mirror that his face is dirty he goes immediately to the well and washes it clean. Likewise when a man of good will sees himself as reflected by the Scriptures...and realizes that his conscience is defiled," he will do something about it.[12]

Service

A third essential spiritual discipline is selfless service to others. Jesus mandated this: "Whatever you did for one of these least brothers of mine, you did for me" (Matthew 25:40). Many people find in service their greatest joy and closest intimacy with God in love. Others do not serve easily.

Service is sometimes thought to require doing something special, like ladling soup in a shelter for the homeless, building a new house for a poor family, or visiting people in prison. These are wonderful forms of service, but they are not the only genuine service. Every kind of sharing can be service.

To begin with, service is an attitude. Like everything else in spiritual effort, motivation is the essence, and activity is the result of the heart's inclination. Service means putting oneself at the disposal of another person's need or well-being and doing it freely and lovingly without concern for oneself. It means a kind-hearted offering of whatever I may have to whatever you may need. *What* that is matters little.

The necessity of serving one another is built into creation. Catherine hears the Lord saying about his gifts and graces, "I have distributed them all in such a way that no one has all of them. Thus have I given you reason—necessity, in fact—to practice mutual charity. For I could well have supplied each of you with all your needs, both spiritual and material. But I wanted to make you dependent on one another so that each of you would be my minister, dispensing the graces and gift you have received from me."[13]

Service is love in action, selflessness in action. The activity one performs or the person who receives its benefit is not the main point. A parent serves the children in a myriad of ways. That's just everyday necessity, you may think. To make it genuine service, as a spiritual discipline, do it selflessly for love of God and offer it to God in your heart.

By so doing, you can turn anything you do for another's benefit into service that will bring you closer to God. In most ordinary lives, the daily round includes many activities that benefit someone else. Catherine says that "everything you do can be a prayer...because of the way you use the situation."[14] Let daily chores help your spiritual life by doing them with a generous and free attitude of love and by offering them to God. It is so simple to say in the heart, "Lord, this report is for you" or "Lord, this soon-to-be-clean living room is for you" or "Lord, this cup of coffee for my spouse in bed is for you, too."

When we do everything consciously for God, how can God seem far away? Try it. Make a game of it if you like. Undertake nothing without offering it to God in your heart, and you'll become more aware of God's loving presence in you.

PRACTICE DAILY AND PRIVATELY

In general, spiritual practices are strongest when they are daily, private, and persistent.

Of course, anything we offer to God brings us closer to him. Yet we are *practicing*—and practice is most effective when it is done every day. That is true of any skill to be learned, it is true of relating to other people, and it is true of God. It is better to take fifteen minutes every day to be with God in some conscious way than it is to take an hour and forty-five minutes one day a week. The idea is to permeate our being with awareness of God, and daily experience, daily reminder, daily effort, do it best.

Spiritual practices are primarily between ourselves and God. This does not mean we should never share from our experiences or from our hope and our faith. It does mean that we should not try to involve others in our particular times with God nor should others expect us to do exactly what they do for closeness to God. Each of us must find and follow our own inner guidance and do the practices we individually are most drawn to.

This is especially true in marriages. We are often tempted to want our spouse to relate to God the same way we do, but it is not always fruitful. "It is important to realize that in the interior life we must never take our own experiences (or lack of them) as the norm for everyone else."[15] God draws each of us in the way we are best suited to come to him, and rarely does one of us know precisely what is best for another. If partners do want to share some of their disciplines, they can agree on a special time for that. Each one should still have his or her own relationship with the Lord, however.

Privacy also means solitude, so we may move and speak freely when we are with God. It means that we do not usually race to tell another person what just happened in our prayer. The ego-centric me can so easily steal the good from my experience by claiming it for "me," so it is best not to exhibit it too freely to other people. When we do share something from our interior life, we give all credit to God. In that way, we safeguard that most precious of relationships. Jesus gave us good advice: "When you pray, go to your inner room, close the door, and pray to your Father in secret" (Matthew 6:6).

CHURCH

Spiritual disciplines also include our involvement in Church. Certainly, participation in the sacraments is a practice that bears great fruit in our inner lives—*if* we enter into it consciously and with love. Like everything else, it serves us only to the degree we are inwardly aware and allow it into our hearts.

In Meister Eckhart's day, how often one should receive Communion was a big question. We should perhaps be asking the same, though from the opposite viewpoint. Then, people were accustomed to receive rarely; we, as often as we go to Mass. Each habit has its advantages and its pitfalls.

Eckhart urged that one's "love for the blessed sacrament and for our Lord ought to grow in him more and more, and that his reverent awe for it should not decrease because of his frequent receiving...then the oftener that you go to the sacrament, the better by far will you be...for it is in him that you will be warmed and kindled, and in him you will be made holy, to him alone will you be joined and with him alone made one."[16]

A fine practice is the effort to hear and absorb every word of the Mass. It is so familiar, yet that familiarity is a challenge to our attentiveness. If we can stay alert to the repetition of words, we are helped in our attention to God.

More than that, the Mass is filled with helpful hints about our relationship to God, then climaxed with an act—receiving Communion—that can become a most intimate expression of that relationship. Offering ourselves with the gifts at the offertory of the Mass is consistent with all other offerings, gathers them into one, and presents them tangibly to Christ.

Likewise, all the sacraments are excellent supports, integral to our journey, especially if we bring them into our heart where God also is.

Another part of Church life is participation in shared activities with other Christians. Some parishes are more active than others, but if we wish, we can find a place for participation that serves us individually and also serves the Church.

Many people are already well acquainted with the benefits of participation in sacraments and Church life. We deepen those benefits when we include them in a life increasingly concentrated on God and God's life in us.

CONSISTENCY

Spiritual practices become strong when they are consistent over time. We would not conduct a job or a courtship on an on-again off-again basis, would we? It may not be useful to promise to do something every day for a year, because promises often make for personal resistances. But it is good to ponder, when we begin a practice, whether we want it enough to continue. If so, then we can help ourselves stay with it by deciding each evening if we are going to do our practices on the morrow. Then abide by our decision.

Everything in the section titled "Attitudes to Be Cultivated" (page 69) about perseverance will help us be consistent in our daily practices.

There are many more spiritual practices. The ones we have just discussed—prayer, spiritual reading, selfless service, and participation in Church life—are basic. They are also accessible to everyone and minimally dependent on circumstances.

CONCLUSION

No one can tell you precisely how to look within, to practice, and to offer each circumstance of your life to God. You can get ideas from books and from people, you can experiment to discover what helps you most. It is only in conscious engagement in our circumstances, however, intending to deepen our relationship with God, that we can find what helps and what does not help.

A moment's reflection will show that all the areas of life just discussed are barely touched here. It has been my aim to stimulate your own thinking and to give several points for possible action. When you take action, the book is no longer the teacher. God guides us through our own experiences and efforts.

If you do not see how some particular thing in your life right now can serve your spiritual desires, then go on a search—in yourself, in conversations, in books, in prayer, and in experiments. God does not abandon us just because we do not know something. He helps us find out what we need to know. His grace gives us the strength to do it, too.

Practicing for love of God in all the activities and demands of daily life will not be easy—not nearly as easy as writing about it! Let's not expect ease. Let's expect challenge and gather our resolution to meet that challenge. Let's not expect instant results, either. After all, it took us years and years to develop the habits we have; it will take awhile to change them.

Amma Syncletica knew how life and practice go, and she encourages us. "In the beginning there are a great many battles and a good deal of suffering for those who are advancing towards God and afterwards, ineffable joy. It is like those who wish to light a fire; at first they are choked by the smoke and cry, and by this means obtain what they seek, so we also must kindle the divine fire in our selves through tears and hard work."[17]

Our loving Lord stays close. Little by little, God guides us into greater awareness of his constant presence and constant love. Our part is to be willing to cooperate however we can now see to do. Then do it!

Notes

1 *Sayings,* p. 129.
2 *Sayings,* p. 37.
3 *Scivias,* p. 51.
4 *Maximus,* p. 62.
5 *Sayings,* p. 148.
6 *Sayings,* p. 64.

[7] *Maximus,* p. 63.

[8] *Evagrius,* p. 78.

[9] *Cloud,* p. 48.

[10] *Cloud,* p. 56.

[11] *Cloud,* p. 93.

[12] *Cloud,* p. 93.

[13] *Catherine,* p. 38.

[14] *Catherine,* p. 15.

[15] *Cloud,* p. 141.

[16] *Eckhart,* Colledge and McGinn, p. 271.

[17] *Sayings,* p. 193.

Challenges and Obstacles

I n their writings, the mystics often may seem to overemphasize the negative: what we do wrong or sinfully. Their readers may sometimes feel hopelessly inadequate and vaguely guilty, even when they know they have no real reason to feel that way. It may even seem as if Christian mystics write primarily about sins and miseries. Why would people who know the joy of the Lord want to focus so much on apparently negative experiences?

One reason may be that the mystics assume something we do not always assume: that the reader wants union with God more than anything else. As we have experienced, without this aim, the discussions of all that is "wrong" with us can be moralistic and repressive. With this aim, however, the reading changes quality and becomes neutral instruction.

Let's take the example of a concert musician again. If I want more than anything to play the piano masterfully, my teacher might encourage me in what I do well. But she is certainly going to lean more heavily on what needs improving, on what is preventing mastery, on what I am doing that is not useful to my goal. Such instruction is not about morals. The teacher is cooperating with the student's own desire and purpose.

It is exactly the same in spiritual development. We need to learn as much as we can about what we can do more effectively.

Another reason for the mystic's emphasis on "negativities" is that the more purehearted one becomes, the more obvious and intolerable one's remaining impurities seem. To a person mired in mud, a cupful more will not matter much. But to a person just showered and dressed in white, a cupful of mud can seem catastrophic. The mystics, although they might deny it, all wrote well after a good shower of the Spirit!

A third reason for emphasizing the discussion of difficulties is that difficulties are common to everyone. We can dream of the goal in God adequately enough to set us on the path, and we go on developing our vision as grace is given to us. But the obstacles along the way may not always seem clear. They are not easy to surmount. That is why much time is given by the mystics to looking at the problems, understanding them, and providing clues to overcoming them.

Furthermore, our "negativities" are rooted in our ego-centrism or in our woundedness. We need to be healed, and our ego must be ousted from its domineering position. In cutting away negative tendencies, we work directly toward both. When we are healed and ego-free, we will be able to receive all of God.

Following the mystics' example in this section, then, we look at obstacles and challenges to our spiritual growth.

Before going on, though, please recall the mystics' assumption that underlies this book: that you have said yes to the journey inward to God and that you *want* to examine the obstacles before you. If this is not true for you, this section could increase your feelings of guilt unnecessarily.

Because most of our obstacles lie within ourselves, they are quite painful and embarrassing. At the same time, this makes them accessible to our efforts to overcome them. Some of our experiences actually block further growth, and these must be eradicated or changed. Other experiences that seem to be obstacles are actually steppingstones, albeit big ones. We grow by stretching ourselves to get over them.

In most Christian mystical literature, obstacles are called sins. I choose to avoid the word, not because sin is not real but because the word is so terribly loaded with unhelpful associations for most of us. While it is accurate to say that any inner condition that keeps us from union with God is sin, we usually automatically take "sin" to mean a broken commandment, some deed that is wrong. On occasion, the mystics mean just that, but for them, "sin" usually means whatever remains between them and total union, no matter how small it seems to us beginners. So I find the word *obstacle* or *challenge* more useful for us and more consistent with the intent of most mystical writers.

In a sense, the whole "way we are" at the beginning of our journey is an obstacle. Union with God both requires and bestows total transformation of our being, our whole way of being in the world. We are not able to receive that now. Still, at our core *is* the Image of God, and our aim is full deification, full union with God. The contrast between what we are at the center and what we are in our living causes us to experience ourselves as inwardly split. That split cries out for healing. We overflow with gratitude when we realize that healing is the nature of the journey.

SELFISHNESS

As we are right now, we live with ourselves, rather than God, at the center. That fact encompasses everything else. It is felt in all our choices and activities, colors every experience, and makes many of our responses mechanical rather than conscious and deliberate.

"People say: 'O Lord, how much I wish that I stood as well with God, that I had as much devotion and peace in God as others have,'...or 'Things will never go right for me till I am in this place or that or till I act one way or another'...In fact, this is all about yourself and nothing else at all. This is just self-will, only you do not know it....There is never any trouble that starts in you that does not come from your own will."[1] Meister Eckhart was, indeed, a master at telling us exactly how it is.

If this book is interesting to you, you (like me, as I write it for my own growth) are not yet fully centered on the Lord. We are working at it. We are gradually detaching ourselves from ego-centricity and concentrating on God more and more. We will only arrive when we arrive.

Selfishness usually takes some form of self-indulgence. A me-and-my-desires attitude determines much of our living; it certainly is the root of all our difficulties in growing toward God. Maximus calls our selfishness "self-love" and here is what he has to say about it:

> From [self-love] are begotten the three capital thoughts of concupiscence: gluttony, greed, and vanity. From gluttony the thought of fornication arises; from greed, that of covetousness; and from vanity, that of arrogance. All the rest follow one or the other of these three: the thoughts of anger, grief, resentment, sloth, envy, back-biting, and the rest. These passions bind the mind....The beginning of all passions is love of self, and the end is pride.[2]

It sounds tortuous, doesn't it? Are we so tangled? Probably!

We often become anxious when confronting selfishness because we know that facing it will mean change in our way of living. It will involve more and more denial of our easy indulgences. We're not so sure we want that; and a voice in the mind may wonder if it isn't a little crazy.

Do we consider an athlete or a dancer who refuses pleasures, diversions, and attractive possibilities to concentrate on training to be crazy? Do we call a medical student who works twenty hours a day during an internship crazy? No, we say these are dedicated people, resolved to attain their goal. We admire them for it. Is our goal in God any less valuable than theirs? Indeed, how much more beautiful is a life ordered around God at its center!

All self-indulgence hinders our progress because it puts "me" at the center of my world. As long as "me" is at the center, God will not be, and we will experience ourselves as separated from him. When we are full of ourselves, God can hardly fill us with himself. Bernard speaks strongly about self-indulgence, too. "For the Holy Spirit teaches only the truth and has nothing to do with the life of a man who lacks self-discipline."[3]

Self-indulgence weakens the will; it makes us soft inside. Our will is our source of power to follow Christ. Without it, we will wander aimlessly along, living automatically instead of intentionally. Life on automatic is determined by our desires. When our desires are not controlled by our will, they are like runaway horses, pulling us behind them in a cart with no driver. Who has not said, "I do not need pastry," only to wheel into the next bakery? How did that happen? It happened as a result of desire, uncontrolled by the will. All our desires have a similar effect when the will is softened by self-indulgence.

Maximus tells us that "there is nothing evil in creatures except misuse, which stems from the mind's negligence."[4] Negligence here means neglecting our will, our decisions, in favor of indulging our desires, many of which are rooted in the senses and other aspects of the body.

Maximus continues, "When a person loves someone, he is naturally eager to be of service. So if one loves God, he is naturally eager to do what is pleasing to him. But if he loves his flesh, he is eager to accomplish what delights it. What pleases God is love, temperance, contemplation and prayer. What pleases the flesh is gluttony, intemperance, and what contributes to them."[5]

We can all find plenty of examples in our own daily life. The root question, when we ponder our own indulgences, is how much we love God, how much we are homesick for God. Do we desire God more than these?

Self-indulgence means that our attachments to everything except God will grow stronger, while our concentration on God will be much slower in coming. If we want God deeply, we will—little by little— practice living for that aim and letting self-indulgences fall away.

"The one who loves Christ thoroughly imitates him as much as he can. Christ did not cease to do good."[6]

Some of our desires may be so strong that they require direct eradication. If necessary, we cut them off. That is what Jesus meant when he said, "If your eye causes you to sin, tear it out and throw it away" (Matthew 18:9). He meant not physical mutilation but resolute doing away with self-indulgence of all kinds. Eventually, every bit of it will go. Maximus reminds us of the reason for this stringency: "The whole purpose of the Savior's commandments is to free the mind...and bring it to the love of him and of one's neighbor, from which there springs the splendor of holy knowledge" of God.[7] Sometimes drastic action is required.

Ultimately, our aim is to pray honestly as Eckhart urges: "The best of all prayers [is] 'Lord give me nothing but what you will, and do, Lord, whatever and however you will in every way.' "[8] That may be high above where we now stand, but it is our heart's innermost yearning.

SELF-DECEPTION

Our fundamental self-deception is that we see ourselves as the center of our own world. When we put it into words that way, our reason tells us it is not the truth.

Functionally, however, we do not know it. We experience ourselves basically as individuals separate from others and from God, and we experience life as if it revolved around us.

Our own life does revolve around our own *perception* of it; that much is true. Yet this does not report to us the actual nature of reality. Reality is, ultimately, God and only God. All other "reality" is only "relatively real"; that is, everything but God is transient. Nothing stays the same forever except God. In truth, God is the center of all, and God is at the center of our living. If only we experienced and lived always aware of God centered in God within us! God at the center is the Truth. We want to live in oneness with that Truth.

Anything less than that is a degree of self-deception. It is thinking we are different from what we truly are.

We search for self-knowledge precisely because of this chronic and profound self-deception. As explained in section titled "Attitudes to Be Cultivated," when we truly know ourselves at our very center, we will know the Lord. Then our self-deception will no longer exist. The Lord will be everything for us experientially, inexpressibly more important to us than our little ego-self.

All our inner bad habits and the inner enemies of our life with God revolve around this fundamental self-deception, this basic perception of myself as my center. Greed is wanting a great deal for myself. Envy is desiring for myself what others have. Laziness circles my own comfort. Discontent is always wanting more for myself. Pride in all its forms is just another way of asserting that I am the center of importance. Anger and grief and fear—all are self-centered and self-focused.

Every one of these forms of self-deception, often called vices, is the opposite of one of the attitudes we wish to cultivate. Not all of them are discussed in this book, but a moment's reflection will show that greed is the opposite of generosity, laziness is the opposite of disciplined effort, pride is the opposite of humility, and so on.

When we mobilize our will to do battle against all forms of self-deception and selfishness, we know we are in for a long fight. At the outset, it may help to know that it is almost impossible to root out one of these inner "vices" by direct action against it. Instead, we gather strength by admitting that the struggle is present in us. We can then watch the struggle, just as we can watch our emotions, and get to know our vices without getting involved in them. In this way, we strengthen ourselves and weaken the vice. In prayer, we take it to God, offer it to him, beg him to remove it from our heart.

Then we set ourselves to practice the opposite attitude. If we have observed that we are greedy, we can give away possessions to those in need. If we see that we are envious, we can pray for even more goodness for those we envy and deliberately rejoice in their good fortune. If we know we are lazy, we can design disciplines for ourselves. We can do this in our thoughts, which is the most important place to battle inner enemies. We can also fight in action; for example, sometimes a generous act is more accessible than a generous attitude, but both carry us away from self-centeredness.

Of course, if we wish to remove all self-deception, we will be honest with ourselves about what we do see, what we do already know. If we lie to ourselves at the rational level, escape from the fundamental self-deception will elude us even further. In rigorous honesty with ourselves and with God (who already knows it all anyway), we will come gradually to own our own souls.

Yes, it will be painful and embarrassing sometimes, and sometimes remorse will overflow our hearts. These are good, no matter how they feel. They loosen the bonds that tie us to the ego-centered life. They open us to real freedom to know ourselves, as we are, at our very deepest center. There God is, and divine peace and sacred joy and universal love. There is transforming union with the longed-for of our heart.

Hildegard points out the way for us:

> O person, be careful. When you do not look back to God's charity which made you free, when you do not notice the good things God weighed out for you, or when you do not pay attention when God calls you…then you choose death rather than life. If you would call back to mind the Scriptures and the doctrines which the ancient and faithful fathers gave to you, you would avoid evil and do good.… Then God would support you with kindness and would place you in God's bosom, embracing you sweetly.[9]

NEGATIVE EMOTIONS AND
PSYCHOLOGICAL ISSUES

When we think of the qualities associated with life in God—peace, joy, love—we are almost immediately aware of the prevalence of negative emotions and habits in our own experience. So easily, we feel fearful or angry or lost or inferior or guilty.

Negative emotions are natural and ordinary. They are NOT morally wrong. But they surely do get in our way; they are powerful enough to steal our heart from God. Speaking of one of them, Evagrius says, "One who loves true prayer and yet gives way to anger or resentment...resembles a man who wishes to see clearly and for this purpose he scratches out his eyes."[10] How, then, can we work inwardly so that anger and all the rest have less power over us?

First, let's look at what *not* to do. We must not deny that we have negative emotions, and we must not repress them, that is, stuff them away out of our awareness. If we think these emotions are morally wrong, we are likely to deny having them or to refuse to be aware of them. Psychologists warn us rightly about the dangers of repression or denial.

That is not to say that we need ever approve negative emotions. Abba Isidore said that "for forty years he had been tempted to sin in thought, but that he had never consented either to covetousness or to anger."[11] A remarkable achievement! We notice to our encouragement, though, that the temptation itself is not a hindrance; only our consent would hinder us from being close to God. That is challenge enough!

Let's recall what was said about emotions in "General Principles of Spiritual Life" (page 27). Emotions are as changeable as the weather, if not more so. Remember how easily your emotions go up and down with every stimulus.

Second, we are not our emotions. They are profoundly connected to the body's reactions, and we experience them. Who, then, is the experiencer? Who observes and can say, "I feel afraid"? The larger self is the observer, the knower of our experiences. That is ourself. Emotions are only a part of us and not the most powerful part, either, unless we identify with them.

When we identify with our emotions ("I am angry" or "I am scared—I can't help being me"), we hand over to changeable emotions the power in our whole personhood. The slightest progress in self-knowledge will show us that we *have* emotions. *We,* however, are more.

The Desert Fathers and Mothers knew it, too. That's why they believed that a life without negative emotions is possible, and they strove to attain it. Abba Poemen said, "God has given this way of life...to abstain from everything which is contrary to nature, that is to say, anger, fits of passion, jealousy, hatred and slandering."[12] These emotions are contrary to our deepest nature. While they are usual enough, they are not what we most profoundly *are*—the Image of God in Christ Jesus. Can you imagine Jesus being plagued with such emotions?

With just a small edge of awareness, we will know for ourselves that, although we may habitually allow them to inundate us, our emotions are not our *self.* In that recognition, we are no longer so completely under the powerful influence of the emotions.

Third, we recall that emotions do not always tell us the truth. We may not have considered the implications of that fact for spirituality— or even for effective living in general.

Here is one example. My husband and I had planned to climb Angel's Landing, a huge rock outcropping in Zion National Park. We hiked to the point where the trail moved onto the outcropping and snaked its way around. From where we rested, the nearly vertical-looking sides of the rock swept down farther than I could see. Terror arose in me. Nothing I told myself changed the fear: "The Park service wouldn't allow it if it were so dangerous; the trail is built for ordinary hikers; hundreds of people have done it—there comes someone down now!"

The fear told me my life was at stake. My mind couldn't make the fear go away. What to do? Well, by this time in my life, I had already decided that fear would make no more decisions for me when I knew it was lying. So I stood up, used the adrenaline for climbing—and went to the top. I knew the emotion was not the truth and it was not myself, so I could choose a larger view, neither denying the fear nor squelching it but deciding in the will how to act.

Emotions are usually like that to some degree. We react, but our emotional reaction may be a lie in the face of the real situation. We are buffeted by emotions until we learn to use our will to follow what we know to be true. It is as if we acknowledge the presence of our inner obstacle, then walk past it, continuing on our chosen path.

Let's say anger arises inside us. Do we fly into expressing it? It is not necessary; some studies have shown that expression can increase emotion. Rather, we acknowledge its presence ("Hello, anger, I see you") and then try to stay aware of it, watching it rage on within us. Easy? Not at first. Possible? Yes. And empowering and healing, too.

In this way, we will follow the promise of Maximus: "Purify your mind of anger, resentment, and shameful thoughts, and then you will be able to know the indwelling of Christ."[13]

Watching our emotions is a kind of self-observation. It is not denial, and it will not harm us. It may require all the willpower we have available, especially the first few times. But everyone can learn to do it. If we stare at emotion, it will gradually dissipate. The same is true of any emotion: face it, let it rage around in you, under your observation, and it will gradually go away because it is totally changeable in nature. Do not feed it, do not deny it: watch it.

Then, when the emotional energy is quieter, offer this negative and unhelpful habit—for emotions are learned habits, often from childhood—to God and pray the Lord to take it away. Sacrifice it on the Lord's altar in your heart. "Prayer is the seed of gentleness and the absence of anger, [and] is a remedy against grief and depression," as Abba Nilus said.[14]

Watching our emotions will also give us clues to our deeper difficulties. Evagrius, the consummate psychologist among the Desert Fathers, advised that we learn to "recognize by which emotion you are more inclined to be led astray, and employ your whole strength in pleading with God" to take it away.[15]

Sometimes such prayer will be a sacrifice; we tend to be strongly attached to our emotions. It doesn't seem to us that we like negative emotions—although some of us actually do like them. We cling to them, feeling justified in our anger or our fear, "knowing" that we are horrible people or otherwise capitulating to our emotions as if they were all-powerful.

We are conscious beings who can watch our emotions, and we can choose to identify with that larger watchful consciousness rather than with our emotions. To do so, as an offering to the Lord, is a mighty aid on our inner journey. It is also the truth.

We can practice against negative emotions, too. Maximus points out direct antidotes: "Fasting, hard labor, and vigils do not allow concupiscence to grow...with anger: long-suffering, the forgetting of offenses, and meekness check it."[16] The practice of the virtuous attitudes takes negative emotions away, though hardly immediately. Evagrius says that detachment from pleasures helps avoid anger, as will detachment from all desires. He advises us, upon the arousal of such emotions, to go directly to prayer for help.

Again, a word about lifelong emotional issues stemming from childhood causes: psychotherapy is sometimes helpful. If you need it, get it. Offer the therapy also to the Lord as a sacrifice for your inner healing that will enable you to get on with your relationship to God. If you truly long for God, however, please do not stop with therapy. Remember that therapy is not the same as spirituality. The journey to God takes us far beyond therapy.

DISPERSION OF ENERGIES AND ATTENTION

Since the central shift in spiritual growth is away from the changeable and toward God, we can see that throwing our attention and energies into all sorts of activities and directions is counterproductive. If someone who wants to be a doctor spends seventy-five percent of the time gardening, fishing, or traveling, the goal will never be achieved.

The other evening I saw this clearly—again—in myself. I felt quite inspired by something I'd read, but instead of using that inspiration to go apart and pray, I found myself picking up irrelevant reading material just for diversion. Television-watching is a big culprit for many people. Window-shopping is another. We dump energy in huge quantities doing that, as any shopper knows when he or she gets home.

Coffee-klatsching can be another, as can gossiping around the food-vending machine at work.

There are millions of diversionary activities, and we all use them. They are really enemies of our union with God, which requires increasing focus on God. They steal our life-energies from our deepest longing. If we are worn out from scattering our energies on things that we don't even care about, how can we expect that our time with God will be alert and loving? Relationship with God takes energy, and receiving God's spirit and spiritual gifts requires alertness. The dullness of overused diversion prevents us from knowing God.

Furthermore, dispersion of energies means dispersion of attention. Why is contemplation—direct knowledge of God—so difficult? Because we are habitually overstimulated and we habitually have brief attention spans. If something isn't shouting at us, we have difficulty remaining alert to it. Our attention is already wandering to some stronger stimulus. So whenever we try to be interiorly silent for deeper prayer, we find ourselves terribly fidgety inside.

We need not berate ourselves for our dispersion; we come by it naturally. It is part of our culture. We may wish, however, to live differently so we can learn to attend steadily to God within us.

Among the many practices we can undertake to help ourselves, here are two: First, we can practice attending fully to whatever we are doing. Second, we can make decisions about activities in the light of their effect on our attention and energy expenditure.

To attend fully to each activity, we will constantly be drawing our mind back to the matter at hand. The mind will go dancing off like a drunken monkey careening in the jungle. Our will is stronger if we do not force anything but simply remind ourselves to attend to what we are doing. We want to practice being fully present to each moment—concentrating totally on the task at hand or giving ourselves wholly to enjoying our play.

Full attention is undivided. So often, we do one thing while thinking of another. We mow the lawn while thinking of the problems at work; while at work, we dream of traveling. We can always practice attending to what we are doing and doing with our whole selves only one thing at a time. Then when we turn to God, we will be better able to attend to him as well.

We may find that certain activity scatters energy and attention so wildly that we have great difficulty returning to alert awareness. Then we may decide not to pursue that activity anymore, even though there may be nothing wrong with the activity in itself. When it takes our energies and attention away from our own goal, however, we may wish to avoid it, exactly as an athlete avoids certain foods.

A caution: just as each person needs his or her own spiritual practices, so our choices of supportive activities are individual. If we choose to omit certain activities or pleasures, it will not help us to demand or expect that anyone else do the same—and especially not our spouse. Nor should we allow others to determine our activities. A decision made for reasons of our own interior growth is just that, and it may not be appropriate for anyone else. It is counterproductive to think that we know what is helpful for another person. Let's make our own choice for ourselves alone. If the nature of our choice necessarily involves another person, such as wanting to stop square dancing and thus leaving our spouse without a necessary partner, then we want to discern carefully. We may find a way to keep the activity for the sake of a loved one but use it constructively for our own inner purposes, offering it to God in our own heart. Spiritual growth sometimes requires a good bit of ingenuity!

INABILITY TO HOLD GOD'S INNER GIFTS

One of the most common, and most disappointing, experiences in spiritual life goes something like this: during prayer, an experience of profound peace suffuses the heart, along with wonderful understanding and a fullness that is God present. I want to stay there, to live in that inner awareness of God forever. Sometimes it does stay—for an hour, a day, or maybe even longer. But then it leaks out of my heart and disappears. I am unable to hold it.

At times like this, the mystics, being honest with themselves, simply admit their weakness. God, even in these small and gentle "doses," is too much for them to contain. They are prone to pray, "How will I ever be any different unless you make me different?"

We can benefit from their example.

First, we simply accept what has happened. It never helps to try to recapture the experience. It was given and now it is gone; we don't know where or how. But—and it helps to remember this—it has changed us, whether or not we can identify the difference. Nothing God gives is ever without its effect, so nothing is ever lost. It is like filling a hole with pebbles one at a time, over a long period, and eventually the hole will be full. God's gifts, received one at a time over a long period, will make us totally his. We can count on it. God is faithful.

Then we can look to see if we did something that dispersed the experience. Many times we did. How often have we touched divine Love, only to have our habit of faultfinding drive love away from our heart? How often have we been steadied in prayer, only to race into some energy-scattering activity? At such times, the only recourse is to see clearly, ask God for the grace to do it better next time, and go onward.

Our general state of being will affect our ability to keep what is given. Obviously, if our life is filled with dispersion of energy as just discussed, we won't be able to hold much of anything within. If we are deeply involved in many attachments and desires, it will be harder for us to make stable space within for God's gifts of experience. Attachments and desires, clinging to anything but especially to negativities, are the constant objects of our efforts to change. We go on trying to become more detached, less clinging, more willing and allowing.

Maximus knows the problem. He says, "If you have been granted divine and sublime contemplations, pay close attention to love and self-mastery, so that by maintaining your sensitive element undisturbed, you will also keep unfailing the splendor" of your experiences.[17] All our basic efforts toward God will eventually strengthen our capacity to receive and hold God's grace and gifts.

One particular obstacle that many Christians experience is a need to stay in control. We have been taught from earliest childhood to "be good." Being good required considerable self-control right from the beginning, and many of us still exercise it the same way. Consequently, we have so tight a grip on ourselves that opening up and becoming willing to allow God to act within us is a major challenge. The balance requires skill: to stay alert and attentive, while allowing God's work.

We may help ourselves overcome our need to control by practicing attentiveness and willingness, as was already discussed. We can also practice letting go of control and just expressing ourselves spontaneously. We can be outlandish sometimes!

We may spontaneously follow all our loving impulses, our joyful impulses, our playful impulses, doing what we wish and letting the outcome be whatever it will. Your impulses will be unique to you, but here are some I've enjoyed: taking a one-hand swing around a light pole in broad daylight, standing in a lake and splashing with the flat of my hand, hugging someone when they least expect it, whooping in delight over a gift (instead of a polite thank-you).

Perhaps spontaneous open expression and its partner, opening to God, are part of what Jesus meant when he said we must become like children. Children are spontaneous. Overcontrol is not their way until adults teach them.

As our practice continues, we become stronger. As our love for God becomes more and more the center of our daily decisions and activities, we will be more able to open ourselves and remain open to receive God and hold the gift. It is a wonderful prospect.

THE RACING MIND

We have mentioned the difficulty of attaining the steady attention necessary to attend freely to the Lord. We can take encouragement from a basic fact about the mind: it was born to run. We need it running to live in this world. The mind is also an incalculably valuable friend on the spiritual journey.

Yet it can be an obstacle in the same way that emotions are an obstacle; we identify with it and think that our mind *is* us. Like our emotions, the mind is not us. It is a valuable aspect of ourselves but never the whole. We must go beyond the mind to become one with God.

This may sound like saying we must go into a void, and there are moments when the experience may seem like that. But it is never the whole truth. Just as the real "I" is more than the emotions, so I am more than my mind. So are you—much more!

All the practices we do for spiritual development will help to remove the domination of the mind. Gradually, we will learn to use the mind as a servant of our goal in God.

We can observe the mind. We can focus awareness on the mind and learn to watch it as one watches a movie. With practice, the thoughts slow down and eventually become still—for only a moment at first, then gradually for longer periods. A still mind is necessary for our central practice, contemplative prayer. In stillness, we come to know the Lord in our own inner experience. That is why it is so important.

According to the *Cloud,* one aspect of the mind that causes us difficulty is the imagination. The purpose of the imagination is to represent to our thinking the images of things as they are; but it is quite prone to distort things, too. The author points out that it is hard for beginners in the practice of silent prayer to "wrench their minds away from the myriad delightful thoughts, images, and daydreams of their past."[18] Those who have tried to see their racing mind would agree. To counteract these tendencies, the *Cloud* recommends pondering the truths we know and focusing essentially on the goodness of Christ. Then real silence gradually becomes possible.

The ability to act from that inner stillness is also a great asset in the rest of life. For almost everyone, it will be a long time before it is consistent, yet practice and grace will enable us to keep inner silence.

A second way to practice steadying the mind is to ignore racing thoughts, letting them go through the mind and out again, while attending to the silence between them or beneath them. It is not difficult. One fixes the attention on the pause at the end of each exhale. In this pause, no movement and no thoughts intrude.

Such practices require a quiet body and a relatively quiet environment, especially at first. As already mentioned, these practices may be used to enter the silence for contemplative prayer.

Additionally, both practices, watching our thoughts and focusing on the silence between exhale and inhale, can be practiced anywhere if our mind is not immediately needed. Any time we must spend waiting (for the doctor, the movie, the cash register, the lube job, the laundromat), while hoeing the garden or vacuuming the carpets or getting gas, we can turn our attention within and do these practices.

Most people soon find the practice itself delightful because it quickly gives way to an awareness of inner peacefulness and interior love. The overall effects of such practice include one that is especially interesting to lovers of God: the mind gradually ceases to be such an obstacle on the path because we can, within ourselves, as ourselves, go beyond our mind to direct awareness of the Spirit.

To our encouragement, the *Cloud* assures us that "there will come times when your mind is free of involvement with anything material or spiritual and totally taken up with the being of God himself...And at such times you transcend yourself, becoming almost divine."[19] So, we keep practicing.

PROCRASTINATION

In all of our efforts, in all of our progress toward God in our heart, we are confronted by a too-familiar obstacle: procrastination. We think we have all the time in the world and can begin our journey tomorrow or take up the new discipline next week or cut away that habit we know is hindering us—but not now. Next Lent, maybe.

It does little good to tell ourselves that we could die any time. We don't believe it—unless, of course, we reflect regularly on our own death as a meditational practice (an excellent idea). In general, all the reasons why we "should do it now" do little good.

Procrastination is really a form of self-indulgence, and that is why it is so insidious and so inimical to inward growth in God. Procrastination is a vast, common human temptation. We need to understand that procrastination stabs huge holes in our will, weakening our resolve and our interest. It also makes us feel guilty. Guilt is paralysis, which leads to more procrastination and so on forever. How do we break this circle?

One help is to feed our mind constantly with what we know we want. Think about God, dream about the beauty of God, read about the goodness of God, talk about God, sink into the gospels, sing and chant to God (a time-honored practice in Christianity, largely ignored today)—in short, do anything and everything to remind yourself of your longing for God, the yearning that started you on this journey in the first place. If you keep your longing vital and burning, you will be powerfully motivated to do what you can to fulfill that longing—and you know that God will do his part, the larger part.

The second help against procrastination is simple: choose one effort, one practice. Any one from this book would be fine. Choose a relatively easy one, one that attracts you, interests you. Make these first steps as positive as you can and offer your choice to God for blessing and the help of grace. Then do it. Today.

Without berating ourselves for procrastinating until now, we can simply step into another inner place and go for the Lord, the object of our yearning, the only quieting for our restlessness. Rejoice that it has begun!

CONCLUSION

If these are not all the obstacles we will encounter, they are some of the most frequent ones. If our battle to conquer these challenges is successful, we will be much strengthened for any others.

Let us not assume, however, that because only a few paragraphs are given here to each of the obstacles, they will be overcome quickly or easily. For the mystics, lifelong efforts have been required. Our own journey will be no less challenging.

Amma Syncletica was a woman of consummate good sense and long experience. She lists struggles that may be in store: insults and disgrace or pride in praise, illness or pleasures, poverty or riches. Her advice in the midst of all challenges is "do not be discouraged here and now. Rejoice that God visits you and keep this blessed saying on your lips: 'The Lord has chastened me sorely, but he has not given me over unto death.' "[20]

Mercifully, we will not meet all challenges at once. God is infinitely gentle and will guard us against being overwhelmed by obstacles. We may not even recognize those we are not strong enough to deal with. They will be revealed to us when we are ready to overcome them with God's gracious help. "God is faithful and will not let you be tried beyond your strength; but with the trial he will also provide a way out..." (1 Corinthians 10:13).

So to use this section best, go to God in prayer and there take stock of your present inner situation. You will find one obstacle that seems most immediate to you. Begin there. Do not worry about those to come and do not try to work your way into everything mentioned in this section.

One step at a time brings us to the conclusion of our journey. There is no possibility of hurrying—a fact for which we can daily be grateful. So let's try not to jump ahead mentally toward that for which we may not yet be ready.

Last, always and in every case, take the obstacle to the Lord of your heart. Do not ever try to complete these challenges successfully by yourself. You probably could not do it. But even if you could, you would still be in trouble, because the self-sufficient, ego-centric you would take the credit. Pride would rule again. You would be taking backward steps.

As in every aspect of the spiritual life, we must make our effort and then give the whole project over into the hands of God. God gives the results. God in his grace will take away the obstacle when we have been sufficiently strengthened by our struggle.

Be encouraged! Keep the goal firmly in view. Bernard is enthusiastic: "It is a great good to seek God; I think nothing comes before it among the good things the soul may enjoy. It is the first of its gifts and its ultimate goal....What could be better?...What virtue can be attributed to him who does not seek God? What limit is there for him who seeks him? 'Always seek his face,' it says. I think that even when it has found him the soul will not cease to seek him. God is sought not on foot but by desire....Joy will be fulfilled. But there will be no end to desire [for God]."[21]

So instead of being caught in a never-ending circle of self-centeredness, we live freely in a never-ending spiral into God. We are freed by humility and gratitude to live with God at our center. He becomes, then, our very identity, as Paul described: "I live, no longer I, but Christ lives in me" (Galatians 2:20). Only this is true freedom. Only this is true love. Only this is union with the Lord of all.

Notes

[1] *Eckhart,* Colledge and McGinn, p. 249.

[2] *Maximus,* p. 69.

[3] *Bernard,* p. 211.

[4] *Maximus,* p. 62.

[5] *Maximus,* p. 62.

[6] *Maximus,* p. 81.

[7] *Maximus,* p. 81.

[8] *Eckhart,* Colledge and McGinn, p. 248.

[9] *Scivias,* p. 46.

[10] *Evagrius,* p. 65.

[11] *Sayings,* p. 82.

[12] *Sayings,* p. 148.

[13] *Maximus,* p. 84.

[14] *Sayings,* p. 129.

[15] *Evagrius,* p. 32.

[16] *Maximus,* p. 53.

[17] *Maximus,* p. 84.
[18] *Cloud,* p. 132.
[19] *Cloud,* p. 134.
[20] *Sayings,* p. 194.
[21] *Bernard,* p. 274.

Experiences
Along the Way

T oday we Christians are beginning to realize once again that teachings and beliefs are not enough for a true life with the Lord. Many of us grew up with the notion that inner experiences were suspect and that what counted was rational conviction about certain beliefs. We came by this feeling honestly enough. For several hundred years, for strong historical reasons, the Church has been uneasy with mystical experience and with mystics in general. That's why many people today have been taught "Accept the doctrine. Have faith. Don't expect too much now. In heaven, it will be lovely."

Christian beliefs, doctrines, and teachings are vital and necessary aspects of our faith. They originated, however, in experience and are fundamentally intended to support experience. If we have no experience of God and of the inner life that takes us into God's heart, beliefs are sterile. The early Christians, the saints of all centuries, and many Christians whose names never became public discovered Christianity to be a way of life that includes particular experiences of the Lord within their own heart and being.

Bernard writes, "Do not hope to hear from me what reason...discerns. Listen to the inner voice; use the eyes of your heart, and you will learn by experience."[1]

Some of the Church's suspicion of inner experience stems from the recognition that aberrations are possible that can result in misunderstanding and a skewing of life. But a faith life founded only on reason is equally distorted, maybe even more so, because it refuses to welcome or to train our inner faculties. Reason alone is too narrow for the deeper reaches of our being where profound knowledge of God occurs.

No doubt, much true inner Christian living has been taught and nurtured orally instead of in writing, because of its potential for distortion and the tendency to misinterpret experience and teaching. So one who knew God intimately taught one who wanted to learn. That is why spiritual directors have been so important to many mystics—and why we need them today.

Those of us who have begun a serious and dedicated spiritual journey know that the teaching of reason is not the whole of the Christian story, even for otherwise "ordinary" people. People who pray deeply, who seek God with profound openness, *do* experience their lives differently and wonderfully. Their interior, as well as their external experience, is transformed. Let's explore inner experiences. Let's try to understand them in the light of the experience of the mystics who have completed the inward journey before us.

HELP AND PROTECTION

Perhaps from the beginning of one's spiritual interest, but certainly quite early along the way, people experience an awareness of being helped. I don't refer to exterior help, although that often occurs and sometimes quite unexpectedly, even dramatically.

Help comes from within and touches our heart to strengthen us, to encourage us, to keep our longing alive, to bring us understanding, and to challenge us, too. The Holy Spirit is not an abstraction but is alive and active within us. Some of the Spirit's work will go on beyond our awareness, and yet...

Even when we cannot express it exactly, we know that something is gradually being rearranged in the depths of our being. Sometimes the experience of help is quite vivid, arising from our unknown depths, surfacing to our awareness. Sometimes it may feel like a fountain turned on and flowing without our being able to start it or stop it. Sometimes it is much more subtle. It may be a tiny recognition that "I am not the same" or a clear awareness that "I am," that I exist so surely that fundamentally I am safe. Inner help is tailored for the individual, and each one will experience it differently.

We may unknowingly squelch this inner help. If we tend to discount our own thoughts, feelings, and life experiences ("After all, who am I? Nobody!"), we will probably tend to deprecate our inner awareness and experience as well. We may not realize that inner help is God's gift to us. It does not depend on what we think of ourselves.

Once we know that inner guidance, inner strengthening, awareness of love, or peacefulness are indeed a usual part of the spiritual life, we can begin to honor those experiences. We can begin to cultivate reverence for whatever God has done within us. We can give God thanks for our experience. We can begin to use our inner experiences and trust them. If we still feel a little uncertain, we can test them by reading or by sharing with a friend or mentor.

It is better never to think or speak of God's work in us as if it were small. It may seem a tiny change or a small support, but because it comes from God, it will open into infinity if we let it. When we brush any small help aside, we say a small no to the Lord—exactly the opposite of what we want!

As always, we can ask ourselves whether these inner insights and awarenesses serve us well on the spiritual journey. To discern this may not always be easy, yet sometimes we know immediately. We can trust that knowledge. We offer it to God. He will correct it if necessary. If we are doubtful, we can live with the ambiguity, asking God to guide our understanding or to remove whatever does not serve our growth. God is faithful. He will respond and he will protect if we are open to inner changes he makes.

Help also comes from without. People, events, reading, overheard conversations—all kinds of external occurrences seem to conspire to help us along. We learn to watch for them, expect them, welcome them.

Another inner sense enters many hearts early on the way and tells them that they are protected. Protection does not necessarily imply that nothing unpleasant will happen. It does mean that the essence of our journey to God is guarded by the Spirit—and maybe the angels and all saints besides. If this awareness comes to the heart, then it is cause for jubilant gratitude. The way is open, and we can go forward with solid confidence.

Of course, the stream of obvious help is not always steady. Sometimes God does withdraw noticeable assistance in order to strengthen us, as we keep going even when we feel alone. These times are usually not easy—they're not meant to be! They are meant to develop our stability on the journey, our resolve, our willingness for God's will in our life.

During periods when we cannot feel the help we're used to, we can be certain that God has not abandoned us and that God's inner support is still there. The Lord wants us to be stronger in ourselves, so he hides—and sure enough, if we do not allow ourselves to be deflected, we are stronger and braver and more alive when God once again lets himself be experienced more obviously.

HEALING

In familiar descriptions of the "stages" of the spiritual journey, the early one is often called the "purgative way." Many have experienced it as a cleansing of faults or a clearing away of weaknesses.

Today, with insights from psychology, we are inclined to view many of our weaknesses and faults as wounds or hurts that came into our lives involuntarily. From this perspective, we need healing as much as cleansing. And because we need it from beginning to completion of the spiritual way, God will give healing as we are able to receive it and insofar as it serves our relationship with him.

The "how" of healing varies exactly with individual need and receptivity. One form of healing I have experienced and shared with friends who report similar experiences I've not found in the classical writings. Yet it seems common enough and valuable enough to share.

Several different times during my practice of contemplative prayer, a pain or negative emotion or ugly inner tendency has arisen, filling my awareness. Once it was a nameless terror that had been the core of repeated nightmares for half my life. That old terror was suddenly vivid, but I was wide awake. I dared not move, even inwardly. I had learned by then that the Spirit sometimes arouses latent weaknesses, and I did not want to disturb the process. Although the terror seemed to suffuse everything else, I knew it would be all right if I could allow the Spirit to do the necessary work. I sat totally still, watching this terror course through my being.

Suddenly, all was blank. It was so blank that I didn't know it until I came to waking awareness again and perceived the blank spot just passed. The terror was gone. Simply gone. In its place were clean relief and profound quiet. The terror has never returned. The Spirit put me through it one last time so it could be healed forever.

The issue varies with need, being different for different people and for the same person at different times. Many spiritual lives have experienced such a lifting away of deep negativity. If there is any helpful advice when some nameless horror like this appears in you, it is this: Be as still as you can and allow the Spirit to do what is necessary. Trust God. Let the experience come to fullness. You may weep or cry out—that's fine. You will be healed.

THE USUAL "EXTRAORDINARY" EXPERIENCES

In the spiritual life, especially if one regularly practices contemplative prayer, inner events occur. For too long they have been called "extraordinary" and relegated to the great saints or to the insane, depending on one's information and biases. Events like visions (lights, colors, forms), inner sounds (humming, music, voices), strong "knowings" beyond the rational, fragrances, and words—all these and more *do* happen in ordinary people's interior being.

In describing his first such experience, Symeon writes as if it happened to someone else to avoid prideful ego involvement:

> One day, as he stood and recited, "God have mercy upon me, a sinner, uttering it with his mind rather than his mouth, suddenly a flood of divine radiance appeared from above and filled all the room. As this happened the young man...forgot that he was in a house or that he was under a roof. He saw nothing but light all around him and did not know if he was standing on the ground. He was not afraid of falling; he was not concerned with the world, nor did anything pertaining to men and corporeal beings enter into his mind. Instead, he was wholly in the presence of immaterial light and seemed to himself to have turned into light. Oblivious of all the world he was filled with tears and with ineffable joy and gladness."[2]

This experience happened to Symeon, not when he was mature in spiritual life but after only a couple of years of disciplined practice. We may be encouraged to know that even after this experience, Symeon did not then immediately become a saint. In fact, he rather slacked off on his practices and almost forgot the experience for several years. Spiritual maturity comes step by step to all.

There are many levels in human beings. As we pass through them on the way to the Lord at our center, we experience inner events, dramatic or subtle. Again, the type, frequency, and intensity of these events vary with the individual. Some are always "at the movies," with all sorts of inner perceptions, and others never see a thing.

It seems that all the physical senses have interior parallels, and at times these arise, giving experiences of the "inner senses" described by Gregory of Nyssa in the following example (among others in his writing):

"We have two sets of senses, one corporeal and the other spiritual...the smell of the divine perfumes does not proceed from the smell of our nostrils, but from a spiritual faculty which draws in the sweet odor of Christ by an inhalation of the spirit."[3]

People also see inwardly, hear inwardly, and taste inwardly. People experience waves of love or joy or sudden insights. They may discover that they have "powers"—telepathic abilities or the ability to find lost things—or that they are carried into entirely new states of inner awareness.

Such events may seem spectacular, but the fact is that they are widely experienced. People seldom discuss them, either because they have never heard of anyone else who experienced them or they are afraid of them. Having never heard of such events, one does not talk about it, and so on. Furthermore, people are likely to have heard extreme cautions, such as "If you have a vision, call a psychiatrist." More than one of my acquaintances has received just such advice from an otherwise trusted confessor—to devasting effect.

Because inner events are not really so rare and precisely because we may not interpret them adequately, it seems to me that we need to open up about them, giving them some caring attention. If we talk about them, we can surely increase our understanding by exploring them. In this way, we can take the emotional charge off them.

For there is such a charge for many people. They either take such experiences to be signs of "advanced" status on the spiritual journey, or they take them to be indications of "something wrong with my mind." Depending on the individual, inner experiences can seem saintly or dangerous. In themselves, however, they are neither. They mean neither that we are mentally ill nor that we are saints. They are merely experiences along the way. They can, in reality, be useful if we don't go to extremes with them.

Inner experiences can be deeply encouraging. They can offer considerable comfort. They can bring guidance, instruction, and understanding. Julian says, "All the blessed teaching of our lord God was shown to me...by bodily vision, and by words formed in my understanding, and by spiritual vision."[4] Julian spent the rest of her life pondering her visions, praying over them, continually seeking deeper understanding.

Inner experiences can open us to increasing love and to joy in God. Sometimes they are simply beautiful in themselves, like a gift of God shared with a loved one. Sometimes they help the experiencer; sometimes sharing them can help another as well.

Nevertheless, they are not essential to the spiritual journey. They are even commonly regarded as dangerous to the spiritual journey. Why? Because the ego-centric self can grab them for itself and puff up the pride of the experiencer. That shift brings inner growth to a sudden halt. Note, however, that the experience in and of itself does not do this, but the attitude we take toward it can.

The Desert Fathers and Mothers had inner experiences, and they were well aware of their possible ego involvement.

> Another time, Silvanus' disciple Zacharias entered and found him in ecstasy with his hands stretched towards heaven. Closing the door, he went away. Coming at the sixth and ninth hours, he found him in the same state. At the tenth hour he knocked, entered, and found him at peace and said to him, "What has happened today, father?" The latter replied, "I was ill today, my child." But the disciple seized his feet and said to him, "I will not let you go until you have told me what you have seen." The old man said, "I was taken up to heaven and I saw the glory of God and I stayed there till now and now I have been sent away."[5]

Except under duress or unexpected discovery, these Christians did not parade their experiences to avoid taking even the subtlest credit for them.

Inner experiences can also become enormous side trips. If we get attached to these inner events—and they do have their own fascination for many people—they take us away from our aim: the Lord alone. Some people become so attached to them that it is difficult to return to the central path again.

So the question is not whether or not to have inner experiences, for they are not under our conscious control. The question is: if they occur, how can I respond so that my journey will continue?

I have a friend whose quiet prayer is filled with lights and sounds and feelings. At first, they intrigued her, but then she realized she was about to leave on a side trip. So now when something happens, she says to herself, "That's an interesting experience. Keep breathing." And she thanks God, surrenders the experience to him, and continues her prayer. She does not regard them as remarkable, either positively or negatively. She does not try to figure out whether they are good or bad. They are just occurrences that come and go, like everything else except God. When God wills it, they will stop happening.

The *Cloud* admonishes:

> It is so important that we concentrate our whole energy and attention on this gentle stirring of love in the will. With all due reverence for God's gift, it is my opinion that we should be quite careless of all delight and consolations of sense or spirit, regardless of how pleasurable or sublime they may be. If they come, welcome them, but do not rest in them.... When love is chaste and perfect, it may allow the senses to be nourished and strengthened by sweet emotions, but it is never troubled if God permits them to disappear.[6]

Most of us will want to know if such inner occurrences are good or bad for us. The way we can tell is to look at our lives. Do we live better because of these inner experiences? Do they make us kinder? More peaceful? Less stuck in our selfishness? More humble? If so, we give thanks to the Lord. If not, we may prefer to pray that the experiences be removed.

I recall a man whose prayer was filled with lovely visionary lights.

He prayed a lot and loved God dearly. But when his car had a flat tire one day when he was in a hurry, he threw a first-class tantrum in the street.

The spiritual experience, when it is good, has a practical counterpart. The whole aim of spirituality is to know God. Then, knowing God and loving him steadily, we let the fruits of that relationship flow into our ordinary lives and the lives of others. If our lives do not change, something is amiss in our attitude. If our living stays the same, our inner life is incomplete.

Julian writes:

> I am not good because of the revelations, but only if I love God better; and inasmuch as you love God better, it is more to you than to me...for we are all one in love, for truly it was not revealed to me that God loves me better than the humblest soul....For I am sure that there are many who never had revelations or visions, but only the common teaching of Holy Church, who love God better than I.[7]

All in all, it is good to take inner experiences lightly, with a bit of humor if you can. If they are helpful and beautiful, be grateful for them. Let's not take what happens to us with such great seriousness that we endanger our own journey. The most self-serious person is the most ego-centric. That is what needs to change. Don't assume that an experience is important just because it is inside you instead of outside you or because it seems unusual. On the other hand, do not assume that something is wrong if such experiences come to you. If we knew more about them, we might find out that they are about as vital to our love of God as potato salad.

So if you see wings and hear music, say thanks and turn your attention back to God. Do not believe everything automatically; don't discount it, either. Above all, do not fear inner experiences. "Every revelation like this given to men on earth has a deeper spiritual significance and I believe that if the person receiving it could have grasped this deeper meaning in another way, the vision would have been unnecessary," writes the author of the *Cloud*.[8] So, easy does it. Keep going. God is your only goal.

In the end, spiritual life moves far beyond all experiences, except the knowledge and love of God. Bonaventure says it beautifully:

> But you, my friend, concerning mystical visions, with your journey more firmly determined, leave behind your senses and intellectual activities, sensible and invisible things, all nonbeing and being; and in this state of unknowing be restored...to unity with him who is above all.[9]

THE ADVENTURE OF CHANGE

Pursuing God in love, which is spiritual life, will change your living.

Wherever we begin, great glories are in store for us—and we have to change to experience and assimilate them. The spiritual life aims for the highest in God. Its primary by-product is a transformed life, inside and outside.

The changes may be welcome or not, at first. Some people find change quite daunting. Yet we need not be afraid of it. Changes, when they result from interior life, are always good. Sometimes they surprise us. Sometimes we work hard to help them happen. Always they are part of a wonderful adventure.

As we grow toward God, our situations and repeated patterns in life, will be altered. The beginning of spiritual growth is like taking a turn off a familiar road. We are entering new territory, and the scenery will be new, too.

Some people experience change suddenly. From one day to the next, the quality and direction of their daily experience is altered. Desires have shifted, responses are different. Their inner stance is changed. It can be disorienting at first, but it is usually a welcome experience.

Others become aware of change more gradually. I recall the day it dawned on me that my life was no longer under my total control and had not been for a number of weeks. It was a strange feeling, indeed, for one who always tried hard to make sure everything went right. It wasn't that I was lost or my moorings had come loose. It was more as if I had stepped aside from the center of the action and begun to be, just a little bit, the observer. I felt freed. I felt lighter. I felt bemused, but good.

Only later did I learn that this is a common experience. God had begun to take over, and God is supremely free. Therefore, life became fully unpredictable. After I got my breath back, I liked it. It was an adventure to see what God would do next.

It is not as if everything God does is first thought to be pleasant. Challenges and obstacles continue. But many surprises are wonderful. Our kindly Lord trains us as we need it—a little challenge, a little reward, a little test, a little encouragement. It is as if he holds a carrot in front of us to keep us moving—but God will push from behind if necessary.

Changes in circumstances are usually accompanied by changes in behavior and vice versa. Many times we are astonished at our own response to an event or at the words that came unexpectedly from our own mouth. "Was that me?" Well, yes and no. It may not have been the old you. It may mark the beginning of a new you.

We have worked for some changes with great energy, those efforts discussed in this book, for example. Other changes seem to happen on their own. In these, the deep, necessary inner changes have been made by grace beyond our awareness. Then one day something calls forth the new and it pops out, fully ready for expression. It may be a total surprise to us.

As we go along, we may notice that our emotions smooth out; that is, we no longer have such wide swings of mood. We may find that events or words that used to upset us no longer do; they may even seem funny now. We may find that we have increased poise and greater presence of mind when the unexpected happens. Flat tires no longer rattle us. Situations are just situations. We can use them all for spiritual practice and enjoy them for their own sake.

A wonderful story about one of the Desert Fathers illustrates this.

> Going to town one day to sell some small articles, Abba
> Agathon met a cripple on the roadside, paralysed in his
> legs, who asked him where he was going. Abba Agathon
> replied, "To town, to sell some things." The other said, "Do
> me the favour of carrying me there." So he carried him to
> the town. The cripple said to him, "Put me down where you
> sell your wares." He did so. When he had sold an article,
> the cripple asked, "What did you sell it for?" And he told
> him the price. The other said, "Buy me a cake," and he
> bought it. When Abba Agathon had sold a second article,
> the sick man asked, "How much did you sell it for?" And
> he told him the price of it. Then the other said, "Buy me
> this," and he bought it. When Agathon, having sold all his
> wares, wanted to go, he said to him, "Are you going back?"
> and he replied "Yes." Then said he, "Do me the favour of
> carrying me back to the place where you found me." Once
> more picking him up, he carried him back to that place.[10]

Abba Agathon simply responded with love to whatever was before
him. The situation was not an intrusion for him. It was only another
chance to practice his devotion.

A particular change that often occurs is a feeling that we are getting
more ordinary, more normal, less "special," neither specially wonderful nor specially terrible. We may have a vague sensation of getting
smaller and less visible. These are indicators that self-centeredness
has begun to loosen, that we ourselves are no longer so much the
center of our own interest. God has begun to take his rightful place in
our heart.

Whether changes are pleasant or not, they may be marks of our
gradual transformation in the Lord. It is good to examine each change,
seeking to discern whether it supports our journey. Then we welcome
each change, give thanks for every one, and ask the Lord for continuing grace not to waste any of them.

STRUGGLES: VICTORIES AND FAILURES

Sometimes God sends struggles. They may be inner experiences of striving toward him or of wrestling with some issue in ourselves. We may have to grapple with weakness or faults or misunderstandings.

Our struggles may be external. God may hand us difficult or painful situations within which we must live and work and find the Lord and his love. Every life, as no one needs to be reminded, brings its share of difficult times. But for one who longs for God, each difficulty, whether inside or outside, becomes a struggle toward more clarity in our faith and our knowledge of the Lord. Every difficulty has an inner purpose, no matter how totally exterior the issue may seem.

Sometimes in our struggles, we will fail. It may seem as if we were not strong enough or that we did not give enough or that the whole thing was just too big for us. We sometimes fail, too, because we give up too soon. We may not actually "strive with all your might," as Abba Arsenius advised.[11]

Whatever the cause, failure itself can be a wonderful help. If we have given all we know to give or if the situation continues to fall apart no matter what we do or if we cannot solve our inner problem by ourselves, what do we learn?

Abba Anthony said, "I saw all the snares that [are] spread out over the world, and I said groaning, 'What can get through from such snares?' Then I heard a voice saying to me, 'Humility.' "[12]

We can learn humility. After all, we cannot make everything the way we think it should be. If other people are involved, they may choose not to change, no matter what we do. We have our own real limitations. In struggles, and especially in apparent failures, we learn what our limitations are. Our self-knowledge has been enhanced, though we may not find it comfortable.

Real sorrow for being less than we want to be is one of the most potent forces for growth toward God. It sets aside some of our ego-centricity and causes us to reach out fervently for God. Remorse is painful but it purifies. When we experience it, let us not run from it, but quietly allow it to burn out of us what needs to be cleansed. God's hands, like a potter's hands, push us from the outside to shape us but support us inside all the while.

If we have struggled honestly to do and be the best we know, then we are inwardly stronger. We have probably learned more about dependence on God. We may have found afresh God's mercy, God's presence, God's strength, in the very fact that we have failed in our own eyes.

If we think we have failed in God's eyes, too, then we turn to him and seek his forgiveness and the possibility of starting again. It is always given. God always responds to our honest repentance. I have often speculated that if Judas Iscariot had not killed himself but had gone back to Jesus for forgiveness, he probably would have become a great apostle. Often the person who has experienced the greatest forgiveness, or forgiveness for the greatest wrong, becomes a person who loves the Lord profoundly and serves him forever. So we need never hesitate to take our failures to the Lord and ask his forgiveness and his strength for the next challenge.

In some struggles, we will be victorious. We will complete the task or clarify the issue or see the way forward once again. The relationship will improve or some fault in ourselves will be renounced and let go. We will have grown.

Victory is sweet, too. It brings gladness and rejoicing. Let it also bring thanksgiving and a remembering of God. If we called to God even once in the struggle, it behooves us to remember God gratefully in victory. Without God, we would have had no victory. Victory is always gift, always grace.

Victory can tempt us to allow our ego-self to take too much credit. Then, seeming victory becomes defeat at a different level. If we are more prideful than before, victory stops us in our efforts toward our goal in God.

Someone has said that the spiritual journey is like walking on ice; vigilance at every step is required. What seems like a good move may send us tumbling. The inner value of events is not always the same as the apparent value. So always we ask ourselves—and the Lord—what is the deepest gift in this situation? What brings me closer to God?

SUFFERING

Suffering and pain are part of life. Suffering will be a part of the journey to God. If we experience *only* pain, something is amiss. No one has yet experienced union with God, however, without pain.

We tend to be naturally afraid of pain and resistant to it. We do everything we can to avoid it. Some people make a life stance out of their attempt to avoid pain. No one succeeds entirely, though. Suffering comes to all.

When we consider suffering in relation to spiritual life, we want to examine its cause and discover how it can be useful to our goal in God. Suffering has proved helpful to many people on their journey when they knew how to use it. Expending energy to avoid pain is not especially helpful from the spiritual perspective.

The biggest source of suffering is our own clinging to the selfish self. We cling to our ego-centered desires, our habits, our opinions, pleasant circumstances. More subtly, we cling to our resistances to transformation in God. Everyone clings. It is part of the ego-centered self. In Christian tradition, this clinging is usually called attachment.

As we've seen, this ego-centered "I" must sooner or later be removed from its dominating position in us, to give the central place to God alone. But our selfishness will not go happily. My own "me" will struggle. Our ego will probably fight our every attempt to displace it, to make it a servant to our high aspirations. That fight will hurt.

Meister Eckhart puts it the other way around. "In God there is no sorrow or suffering or affliction. If you want to be free of all affliction and suffering, hold fast to God, and turn wholly to him, and to no one else. Indeed, all your suffering comes from this, that you do not turn in God and to God and no one else."[13] Of course, turning "to God and no one else" is the whole purpose of our efforts! If we knew how to do it all at once, we probably would. Instead, we gradually go forward.

In the beginning, the battle to make that turning to God—and the accompanying struggle against resistances—may be obvious. The further we go, the more subtle the resistance of the ego-centric self. We can plan on a lifelong battle with self-centeredness. The fight may not actually go on that long. If it is shorter, however, it will be the merciful gift of God. We may as well assume we are in it for the duration.

The key to making our pain useful and redemptive for us is to practice withdrawing our sense of identification from the pain and placing it in God. That may not be easy, but like many other inner skills, it can be practiced with small occasions. Suffering in itself need never make us unhappy so long as we are able to say, "I *experience* pain" rather than "*I* am suffering." Pain is an experience, not our identity.

Practice is quite accessible with the physical pains we experience: the dental work, the cuts and bruises, the twisted muscle, or whatever. (Chronic or intense pain is, of course, much more difficult and not the easiest place to begin to practice.) With a little experimenting, we can discover that pain is just a sensation—not one we like, naturally, but not the whole of ourselves either. Not even close to the whole of ourselves. When we relax in relation to the pain, then "the pain" has less chance of turning into "*I* hurt."

Sometimes we are given painful experiences precisely so we can learn that we are not the pain, that we ourselves are far beyond it. Then we can practice and learn to place our primary awareness on our real identity as a child of God or our real aim to become one with Jesus. Then the pain becomes a servant to us as we strive for our real goal.

Identification is the difference. To the extent that I experience myself living in God's love and care and to the extent my sense of identity is rooted there, pain is only pain. We may bear the pain, then, as an offering to God. We may ask God to use the pain to lessen our attachment to the pleasant aspects of our life. Then, like all other circumstances, pain can become an instrument to bring us closer to God. God will help us bear it, even while the pain itself is loosening our clinging to ego-centeredness.

Pain used as an offering to God can even bring a certain sweetness with it. This accounts for much of the great courage of God-centered people in physical pain, in terrible situations, or in emotional or mental distress. They stand strong because their sense of identification is elsewhere than with the pain. It is with their larger self, which is focused on God.

As Bernard said about such people, "They were so moved within by the great force of their love that they were able to expose their bodies to outward torments and think nothing of them. The sensation of outward pain could do no more than whisper across the surface of their tranquillity."[14]

Christian tradition has long valued suffering as an effective help toward union with God, especially as we can then join in the redemptive suffering of Jesus. Some have felt that God is to be found *in* suffering, and those who love God wholly say quickly that if that's where God is found, then give me suffering. Few begin with that desire, however. For most of us, suffering is unwelcome, but we will learn to make use of it for God if we can.

A subtle but essential understanding is that suffering and sorrow are not the same thing. As just stated, pain does not need to make us unhappy. Eckhart points out that suffering always includes God because God joins with us in the midst of the suffering. Then our offering of it brings the suffering to God's heart. "If my suffering is in God...how then can suffering be sorrow to me, if suffering loses its sorrow, and my sorrow is in God, and my sorrow is God...as I find pure suffering for the love of God and in God, I find God in my suffering."[15]

Thus, pain is a teacher and a way to God when we do not identify with it as being ourselves. The rewards of this little distance we recognize between ourselves and our pain are many. We become stronger, we lose a chunk of our habitual fear, we discover that we can bear (with God and in God), and we are thus freed. We lose our attachment to the notion of a pain-free life, and we are enabled to go forward into God with or without suffering.

Along the way, we can even practice dealing with our pain by means of humor. All of us have known people who have major illnesses or other painful challenges, yet who find amusement in everything, their pains included. They are able to find humor everywhere because their hearts are centered on God, not on their small selves. These people do not feel sorry for themselves. Rather, they choose to take themselves—and life's vicissitudes—lightly, so laughter is possible and welcomed in the midst of suffering.

There are also people who cling to their suffering. Let's face it. Some people like suffering because the ego gets something out of it. This is most obvious when it takes the form of self-pity—the biggest ego trip of all. But when someone yearns for God, he or she can place personal identification in God or in Christ as a child of God and let the pains come and go as they will, keeping a calm mind. That is beautiful detachment.

Another kind of suffering experienced by lovers of God is the pain that arises from increasing awareness of one's own separation from God. God is actually not distant at all. Yet our experience of ourselves as far away from God is the root of our difficulty. As we love God more and long for God more, we become increasingly sensitized to that feeling of distance. It hurts to be separated from the Source of our being, the Source of all love, for whom we long. It is like the ache of being separated from a dearly loved partner or child—only more so. Eventually, it is much more painful than even that.

The suffering caused by separation is the cross. It is not at all like the suffering of physical illness or difficult circumstances. Rather, it is like a burning coal we carry around inside or wounds in our hands. It reminds us constantly of our aim toward God, of how much we love God and long for God. The pain of it becomes a touchstone of the intensity of our journey. In this sense, the pain becomes itself a prayer, a reaching deep for the Lord.

So there is sweetness in this suffering because even as we experience its pain, it draws us powerfully closer to God, who is all our desire.

It is true: without this interior suffering, no one will go the "whole distance," no one will complete the journey. With awareness of this pain, we will not be able to stop before the end. It is a thoroughly beneficial suffering.

Working with pain and suffering will be challenging but so rewarding. When pain is subordinated to the spiritual journey, taking a long second place after God, it becomes redemptive, like Jesus' pain. It brings healing from the deepest of all wounds: our self-centeredness.

No wonder the mystics have found suffering a good thing! It helps them toward what really matters to them: union with God.

CONFIDENCE

As our journey carries us along toward God, with its mix of effort and grace, rest and experience, help and challenge, we will become more confident.

The word *confidence* comes from the Latin word meaning "with faith." It is especially appropriate for the spiritual life because the confidence we increasingly experience is not self-confidence. It is confidence in God; it is keeping full faith with God.

More and more we will experience what the mystics report. They know that had they been alone, nothing good would ever happen. Their goal is always too much for them by themselves. But they never journey by themselves. They always journey more and more with God. They have seen God heal and comfort and challenge and strengthen. They have seen him hide and reappear only to find themselves closer to him than before. They have experienced great consolations and full-blown obstacles, and God has always mercifully seen them through. So they credit all to God and rest in their confidence in God's faithfulness.

In our beginnings, every step will seem to demand caution. We feel hesitant and self-protective. As we are more and more aware of God, and our selfishness slowly recedes, we are less self-protective because we know God protects us. We hesitate less because we have fallen so often, and God has repeatedly put us back on our feet. We may choose to be prudent but no longer from fear of unpleasant outcomes; they have all happened, and we are still with God.

Will this confidence in God last right to the end? It seems so. In fact, confidence seems to increase. Many times, this is the only thing that carries a person over the last barriers: confidence in God, in God's love and God's faithfulness with us. We beginners can take courage from the fact that many others have gone before us—the whole way—and have found God to be more than worthy of that confidence.

So we can step out as far toward God as we dare, and our confidence in God will grow. It is a marvelous gift. The sooner we depend confidently on God, the better our journey will be for us.

PEACE AND JOY

Peace is not static, and joy is not always emotional. Peace that is God-given is dynamic. It flows from the heart like a fountain. It suffuses all experience so that one's world appears to be the gift it really is. God-given joy does not send us into excitability or euphoria (unless we are too weak yet to contain it). It is a certain brilliance in our heart that spills over into our experience of living. Both are signs of God's presence within us.

Peace and joy attend our way. Even in sorrow, peace can flow. Even in pain, joy can leap up. Angelus Silesius wrote, "Derided and forsaken, enduring pain and toil, denuded, not possessing, my life is filled with joy."[16]

When the qualities of peace and joy enter our life, we may find them surprising. For many, peace is unfamiliar, and joy is all messed up with situations. Some people even feel vaguely guilty at their first experience of peace springing up from within, thinking they do not deserve to feel so good. Sometimes Christians have thought so much about suffering that their experience of peace and joy has been distrusted. Yet who does not long for a peaceful and joyful life?

When peace and joy come from the Spirit of God, they are not in the least dependent on circumstances. People have lived in the midst of the most awful situations, and their inner peace has not been disturbed, their inner joy still bubbled up to expression. The gifts of God are not dependent on whether we think we deserve them or not. Peace and joy are given when God wants us to experience them, when we are able to accept these gifts. "God works continually, a thousand joys He would pour into you at once, if suffer it you could."[17]

How can we not welcome lovely states of experience? Thanksgiving to the Lord wells up in our heart, and thus we are opened even more to the great goodness of God. That goodness we experience as peace in the inward being, joy in the deepest heart of our heart.

We can be certain that if on occasion we lose our joy or forget our peace, either there is work to be done to receive them again or God is teaching us to walk in faith.

The end of our journey will be ultimate, divine peace, truly beyond anything we can now even imagine. The end will be ultimate joy and blissfulness because that is what God is.

When our being experiences God in his joy and bliss, we will understand what Bernard knew:

> There is a song which, in its singular dignity and sweetness, outshines all.... This sort of song only the touch of the Holy Spirit teaches, and it is learned by experience alone. Let those who have experienced it enjoy it; let those who have not burn with desire, not so much to know it as to experience it. It is not a noise made aloud, but the very music of the heart. It is not a sound from the lips, but a stirring of joy, not a harmony of voices but of wills. It is not heard outwardly, nor does it sound in public. Only he who sings it hears it, and he to whom it is sung.[18]

Notes

[1] *Bernard,* p. 69.

[2] *Symeon,* pp. 245-246.

[3] Gregory, p. 156.
[4] *Julian,* p. 79.
[5] *Sayings,* p. 187.
[6] *Cloud,* p. 123.
[7] *Julian,* p. 80.
[8] *Cloud,* p. 123.
[9] *Bonaventure,* pp. 114-115.
[10] *Sayings,* pp. 21-22.
[11] *Sayings,* p. 9.
[12] *Sayings,* p. 2.
[13] *Eckhart,* Colledge and McGinn, p. 211.
[14] *Bernard,* p. 197.
[15] *Eckhart,* Colledge and McGinn, p. 235.
[16] *Angelus,* p. 67.
[17] *Angelus,* p. 115.
[18] *Bernard,* pp. 214-215.

All for Love

I f this book could be printed so it reflected the whole truth at once, each page would have a transparent overlay in which is embedded the word LOVE. Then everything about principles, everything about practices or obstacles or experience, would all be considered through the filter of love. For that is how spiritual life is actually lived—through a filter of love.

Spiritual life, life toward God, life in God—no matter what words we use, it is all about love and for love and in love. Spiritual life begins in God's love, touching our hearts to allure us to himself. Spiritual life is fulfilled in God's love, suffusing and pervading our total being, our total awareness. Then all is love and love is all.

As we have seen, the only reason to enter the spiritual life is for love. Everything else we undertake along the way is designed only to open us more and more to divine love. If we learn ways of living, if we meet obstacles—all these have only one aim and one fulfillment: to live in unbroken awareness and participation in God who is love.

We are beginners, drawn to God by our yearning for him, which in turn has been planted in our hearts by God. Being beginners does not mean we know nothing or have done nothing at all. It means that the journey is long for almost everyone. Its farthest end is hidden by its very brilliance. We feel like beginners and will perhaps for years more. It's as if what is behind us is minute compared to the expanding vision of what is before us in God. Before God, we may be everlastingly beginners.

We can begin. Every suggestion mentioned in this book is available for a beginning. We may start off strongly or weakly, a practice may seem easy or difficult. Whatever we begin with, it will open up on the far side and continue to open until it has no more boundaries, for God is infinite. We discover ever more depth and ever more vision as we go along.

To enter the spiral into God, we need not *be* anything in particular. We need not do any one thing except express our intention to the Lord. We may begin anywhere. So long as we have a little love and a little willingness—no matter how small or sporadic—we may begin with any understanding, any practice. If we honor our beginning and follow it faithfully, God will use it to draw us into the spiral that never ends but that is fulfilled in the heart of God.

The concrete applications of the way will be different for each individual. One who is habitually self-protective will need practices that open her, that expand him. The one who constantly strives and struggles may find it better to relax a bit and discover how to treat himself with more compassion. The one who procrastinates about what she loves may need a stricter discipline until the habit is broken. The emotional person will need to channel those feelings, and the mental person will need to discipline the mind. We are all different, and our spiritual needs will take different forms.

The only sameness that we all share is the necessity of love. We do not think of love as it really is. Love is, after all, not subject to thought. Love is far beyond thought; it is understood more with the heart than with the mind. Love is available in the essence of our being, the innermost center of our heart, where the Holy Spirit dwells awaiting our awareness.

Since we are beginning, we do not yet live fully in that center, we do not express that inner love fully in our lives. We are practicing, so our experience of love is partial. We need not condemn ourselves for that. It tells us that the greatest adventure of human life lies before us. The quality of that supreme quest is love. Our experience of love will deepen without end. God will give it just as quickly as we are able to receive it. For that ability, we practice.

Love, then, is the reason we begin. Love is the reason we continue. Love is the motor, the power for the journey. Love is the goal. Nothing else matters.

We would choose to love God with or without peace and joy. We would choose to love God without a single experience. We would choose to love God because it is beautiful, it is good, and love is ours for the asking. We *do* choose love because it is already our own deepest nature.

Bernard wrote some of his finest work "on loving God." He says love is "an affection, not a contract. It is not given or received by agreement. It is given freely....True love is content. It has its reward in what it loves."[1]

As we go forward toward God, more and more we realize the worth of God's love to us. Eventually, we would pay any cost—even our very selves—to live in full and steady awareness of God's love forever. An Eastern saint said, "I gave all of myself and got all of God. It was a bargain."

"God is the cause of loving God....He himself provides the occasion. He himself creates the longing. He himself fulfills the desire. He himself causes himself to be such that he should be loved....His love both prepares and rewards ours. Kindly, he leads the way. He repays us justly. He is our sweet hope. He is riches to all who call upon him. There is nothing better than himself."[2] Bernard knew, as each of us is invited to know, that the whole of the spiritual journey is love.

It is our joy to open up to divine love and allow that love to become the whole of ourselves eternally.

Every one of the suggestions in this book is rooted in love and will be fulfilled in love. No one will undertake anything without love, and so love will pervade everything. No practice is useful unless it expands in us the love that we are and the love that we can become.

Our desire for God is our love for him. Trust in God and contentment in our trusting can only be full if they are grounded in love. They
draw us to love God more for his faithfulness to us. Devotion and
self-offering, even for a flash of a second, are expressions of love from
our heart to God's heart. Reverence for the sacredness of all is really
love for all things, all people, all events. As we learn this in our
experience, we can love more because God loves all without differen-
tiation.

Rejoicing in God leads to loving him more intensely. Loving God
leads to rejoicing. Whatever we learn will open us more humbly to
loving the divine Teacher as well as to loving ourselves more truly.
Kindness, generosity, forgiveness—what are they if not expressions
of love for life, for people? In equanimity of mind, we open naturally
to love, because turmoil is no longer in its way.

Good humor, lightness, and cheerfulness come from a loving heart.
They allow love to flow more freely through us—from God to our
life! In our inner watchfulness, we perceive more and more love,
deeper and deeper and increasingly steady. In the inner silence, there
is only love. We have reached toward God from love, and we are
answered only by love.

All the obstacles we meet, all the challenges we are given, are
overcome by love: our love for God and God's gracious love for us
that expresses itself in the strength and insight God gives. All good
experiences are expressions of a shared love. All unpleasant circumstances are the discipline of a love that dares us to be more like
Christ. Every moment of our lives is an opportunity to know love, to
experience love, and to give love. Each moment is the moment God
pours his love into our hearts.

Since we are beginners, we may not think we love God very much
right now. We may seem to ourselves more like beggars for love. But
if we knew nothing of love, we would not even know we long for God.
God has always loved us, so there is love in our lives from our
beginning.

All of us have tasted affection. All of us have cared about someone
else at some time. Everyone has known a moment, or many moments,

of concern for another being, free of selfish interests. Some love nature, some love animals, some love people, some love music or art—love is to be experienced everywhere because love pervades everything. We need only learn how to perceive it everywhere.

We begin by calling to our awareness the love we do recognize by cherishing that love and nurturing it and doing whatever we can to expand it. Love is love, and its object does not matter. We begin with the love we know already. If we love a flower, did God not create it?

When we experience pain, we can discover that the choice to love God in the midst of that suffering is itself a sustaining power. Love sustains. If we love a pet in the midst of our pain, that love will sustain—not because of the cat or dog but because of the love that is awakened in us. Love is love; love is God, recognized and acknowledged or not. If we do acknowledge it, then the power of love expands without limits.

So if we think our love for God is small, what do we love? A child? A pet? The natural world of beauty? Begin there. Open the heart to that love more and more. Give to that love, express that caring, then turn to God in the midst of it and you will find no difference (except perhaps in concepts, which now do you no further good).

Love will come to you in a million ways, because love, being God, is infinitely inventive. Love seeks you and waits attentively for the slightest chink in your usual defenses. Finding it, love slips into your heart: it is God.

Every idea and every practice in this book is a readiness exercise, a support for more deeply interior realities. If we choose to accept the ideas and do the practices and grow inwardly from them, we will be carried by them to another point of choice.

It may be as if we live in a courtyard right now, being taught and prepared for the day we can pass through a certain door to an interior sanctuary. We cannot enter that sanctuary until we are readied by God's life in us. So we practice now, in the hope that the innermost door, where God dwells wholly, will swing open for us one day.

Yet we are not alone, even in the courtyard. There are others who long for God. More importantly, Jesus said he is the way itself. He is with us from the start, from *this* start, right now. Our consciousness of God's presence may be sporadic now, and our emotions or thoughts may seem more real to us than God does at times. No matter. God is present, Christ is the way, and we have taken a first step by saying yes to the invitation planted by grace in our hearts.

And what will we find in that inner sanctuary? We will find love. In the end, there is nothing else. It is our longing for love, our faithfulness to acting on our longing, and the grace of loving God that will bring us totally to himself, to eternal love.

And so we pray together, from our hearts, with the unknown Jewish mystic who wrote:

> Draw me to you, God, with the breath of love. Swiftly shall I come to stand within your radiance, that I may attain the sweetest of all intimacies.

> My soul aches to receive your love. Only by the tenderness of your light can I be healed.

> Engage my soul that I may taste your ecstasy. My heart yearns with an agelong yearning for the embrace of your compassion, the refuge of your strength.

> O God, who experiences all, penetrate my longing with your presence. Reveal yourself, let loose your light, surround me with your sheltering love, for the time has come.

> Hurry, my Loved One, embrace me that I may rejoice in the Source of all joy.

Notes

[1] *Bernard,* p. 187.
[2] *Bernard,* p. 191.

Appendix

DESERT FATHERS AND MOTHERS
(ca. 250-425)

Imagine living when your Christian faith made you a criminal "wanted" by the government. Moreover, society seemed to be falling apart, with corruption and moral decadence virtually everywhere. If your Christian spiritual life was your top priority, what would you do?

In the early centuries of Christianity, many men and women responded by fleeing into the Egyptian and Palestinian deserts. There they sought God, praying and working in the silence of the vast desert spaces. Even when Christianity was legalized in 311, the desert movement continued and even grew.

Although solitary, these men and women belonged to communities. Mostly, they remained alone in their huts or cells far from their nearest neighbor, gathering regularly (not always weekly) for Eucharist and a day's sharing.

The above dates reflect a period when the Desert Fathers and Mothers were known and visited by people from the outside world. But these solitaires refer back to the "old days" when the desert Christians were much greater than they themselves. So for several hundred years, the desert was occupied by people who sought God in circumstances that, while indeed harsh, may not have seemed as impossible as living a profound Christian spirituality in the midst of an inimical society.

What were they like, these single-eyed seekers of God in the desert? They were as different individually as we are: women as well as men, young and old, from every social background. They had one thing in common: they desired God above all else. They strove to put God first, above every other human tendency. Alone, ascetic, filled with hope but amazingly vigilant to their inner state, nothing in their life was easy.

Yet they were seen by their visitors as men and women of joy, deep devotion, flowing peacefulness, gentleness, and charity. They chanted, they studied, they fasted, they prayed, they rejoiced. They engaged in simple labor, such as weaving palm baskets to sell—less for their own income than to have something to give to the poor. Some walked miles to fetch their own water and more miles to the eucharistic celebration. The Egyptian desert was known as a holy land, filled with happy and loving saints.

The Desert Fathers and Mothers left few writings, but many sayings were collected by their visitors. From these, we learn that these women and men were experts in what we might call "spiritual psychology." They discovered in their own struggles and victories, their own bodies and spirits, how the life-toward-God proceeds and how a person can follow it into the fullness of God. They knew intimately the inner resistances and challenges of every spiritual life. And though they spoke less about their glories, we have enough hints—in their teachings and in their miracles—to know that they experienced God, knew Christ, and rejoiced in the help of angels even while battling inferior spirits.

Their lifestyle may seem extreme to us, and we need not copy it. But we must honor their total devotion and complete determination, doing *whatever* seemed necessary so that God might grant them union with himself.

GREGORY OF NYSSA
(335-395)

Gregory of Nyssa came from a family of saints, including his brother, Saint Basil the Great, and his sister, Saint Macrina. His grandparents had been persecuted and expelled from their homeland for their Christian faith, but the family never wavered. Gregory was born in Cappadocia (modern Turkey).

Well educated and eventually married, Gregory enjoyed secular prominence as a teacher of rhetoric. He was not particularly dedicated to Christianity until the emperor, influenced by Gregory's brother, Basil, appointed him a bishop. Gregory did not want the position, but he could not refuse. It was a turning point for him, though, and he went forward to become a profound mystical saint and theologian.

In the fourth century, Christianity, although legal, was highly controversial and closely tied to government and politics. It became the state religion in 385. This was the century of major Church councils, including Nicea, which hammered out doctrines that still remain today. Of course, the councils had political implications, but their primary criteria for decisions about doctrine were based on questions such as "Is this true to our Christian *experience?*" and "What are the consequences of this for the Christian's spirituality?"

As bishop, Gregory had his troubles. He was accused of embezzlement by the emperor, who disliked all bishops faithful to Nicea's decisions and banished Gregory from his diocese. Gregory used his exile to begin writing. When circumstances enabled him to return to his post three years later, there was widespread rejoicing. Then Basil died, and Gregory shouldered Basil's vision and work. It made of him a deeper man, now fully committed to matters Christian.

Soon favored at court, he wielded great influence on the development and acceptance of doctrine about the Holy Spirit. But public influence fluctuates, and his declined. Once again he used the apparent reversal to better ends, giving his total attention to his own inner spiritual life until his death in 395.

Gregory wrote voluminously, commenting on Scripture, explaining doctrine, arguing about philosophy, and exhorting to spiritual life, which he described in vivid detail. Although he did not write in the first person, many of the spiritual events he records could have come only from his own experience.

Gregory's teaching emphasized the magnificence of active Christian life. Never a monk (he loved his wife enough to take her along wherever he went), he served the Church in the world and participated fully in the searchings that characterized his times. Simultaneously, he yearned for God and loved Christ, himself an example of the infinite growth that spirals inward to our innermost depth, the image of God, the presence of the Spirit in ourselves.

His own words tell us how he regarded his own life: "We regard falling from God's friendship as the only thing dreadful and we consider becoming God's friend the only thing worthy of honor and desire."[1]

Note

[1]   Gregory, p. 137.

EVAGRIUS
(345-399)

Evagrius Ponticus was an early friend and student of Basil the Great, who ordained him a lector. Then he went away to Constantinople for his full education and the intellectual life he loved. He was ordained a deacon by Saint Gregory Nazianzen and enjoyed the friendship of Saint Gregory of Nyssa.

Life was successful and comfortable for Evagrius. He became a much loved and admired member of the imperial court, though remaining a responsible cleric. In great social demand, Evagrius became less interested in prayer and contemplation. Then a crisis came: he fell in love with the wife of a high official. This plunged him into a bitter struggle for self-control. In a nightmare, he was accused of great evil, and he promised to "watch over his soul." The next day he fled the capital and sailed to Jerusalem.

He was welcomed by a profound Christian widow and ascetic, Melania. With her friend, Rufinus, Melania watched over the Christian growth of a double monastic community. Soon Evagrius found a happy place in this dedicated circle. Yet once again life became too comfortable, and he forgot his promise to take care of his soul. Crisis repeated. He became deathly ill, and the physicians could do nothing.

Melania guessed the true cause of his sickness and persuaded him to become a monk. He took his vows in his bed. A few days later, he was well. The next chapter in his story is missing, but in 383 we find him in the Egyptian desert.

It was not an easy environment for Evagrius. His intellect and its habits were not respected or desired by many in the desert nor was his tendency to offer too much unasked advice. He was a stranger in Egypt, but he accepted the blunt reproof of his new brothers and dedicated himself to learning humility and silence. So thorough was his determination and so loving his spirit that he soon became a leader in one of the desert communities.

He continued to be a pupil of men greater than himself. He sought them out, obeyed their directives, and took up extraordinary ascetic practices, living on small amounts of bread and oil. Desperately tempted both sexually and to blasphemy, he struggled valiantly and eventually saw victory. He gave the rest of his life to the inner effort to purify himself fully so he could receive God fully.

Evagrius wrote hundreds of short paragraphs of teachings, a clear commentary on spiritual effort. He tells of experiences and struggles recognizable by anyone seriously seeking experience of God. His advice still holds true, even for us who do not live in deserts or monastic cells.

As his own purity of heart grew and he became a master of contemplation, he also grew in love, showing deep mercy for the troubled and wayward and humble charity toward all. Gradually, his fine intellect became fully a servant to his contemplation, and he received great gifts: prophecy, understanding, freedom from emotion and desire, miracles, and profound peace.

He was ill for some time. At the Mass of the Epiphany, he received his last Communion and died there, content in the Lord.

MAXIMUS THE CONFESSOR
(580-662)

Born in Constantinople, Maximus grew up in the capital of the Byzantine Empire. The times were not peaceful. Political and religious struggles intermingled so completely that one could be accused of treason for holding a religious idea different from the emperor's. Maximus was bright. His boyhood education was broad and challenging, and his later writings show acquaintance not only with Scripture and the Church Fathers but with Greek philosophers as well.

When Maximus was about thirty, he became secretary in the court of the Emperor Heraclius but resigned about three years later to become a monk. He remained a lay Brother all his life. He gave his reason simply: he loved the monastic form of spirituality and wanted to seek only God.

In 626 he left Constantinople, pressured by military events. We know little of his wanderings, but he arrived in North Africa probably in his forty-eighth year. For twenty-five years, he wrote and disputed on theological subjects of highest importance to Christian understanding, both in doctrine and in spirituality. But any person who participated publicly in such controversies was at serious risk.

Eventually, Maximus visited Rome, where he supported Pope Martin in a famous argument about whether Christ had one will or two—hardly an exciting subject to twentieth-century Christians. But it was desperately important to Maximus; he was devoted to announcing the truth as he was given to see it, and he believed the outcome had large implications for spiritual life. He did not count the cost to himself in such struggles.

The cost turned out to be high. The Byzantine emperor arrested both Maximus and the pope, tried them for treason, and banished them to Thrace. Even there, however, Maximus continued to proclaim the truth he knew and in 661 was brought back to Constantinople— eighty-one years old and in chains. There he was tried again and condemned. His tongue and right hand were cut off because he had used them to disagree with imperial authority. Exiled again, he died a few months later on August 13, 662. Nineteen years later, he was vindicated and honored.

His title, "The Confessor," refers to his persistence in confessing the Christian truth for all to hear, steadfastly until martyrdom.

For us, his teaching about spirituality is more immediately useful than his doctrinal subtleties. He taught that a human can be deified by grace and gave considerable instruction about how a person can cooperate—*must* cooperate—with that amazing process. All his teaching about the virtues, offered in writing in great detail, is set in this framework. Though his instructions do not imply a systematic progression, it is clear that imitation of Christ is the way and that it must be so thorough that eventually one can actually love all people equally. For Maximus, morality—the practice of virtues—is a means to a far higher end: deification, total union with God, sharing in the life of the Trinity—all offered to the Christian because of the Incarnation.

SYMEON THE NEW THEOLOGIAN
(949-1022)

More than any previous Christian mystic and theologian, Symeon tells us about his own interior life—a blessing needed in his own century as in ours.

Symeon was born in Asia Minor to noble parents. He finished his secondary schooling in Constantinople. Then suddenly, at fourteen, he decided he would study no more.

He had met someone, a saint he came to believe, who agreed to teach him and be his spiritual father. This man's name was also Symeon, called the Studite because he was a lay monk in the Stoudion monastery. The teenager was given a few instructions about prayer and a book to guide him. He worked long days managing a patrician household and in the evenings gave himself to prayer and reading.

Gradually, his practices increased until they were continuing until midnight. But his work did not flag: up early for matins, and he was on the job.

Six years later, Symeon's first — and totally unexpected—spiritual experience occurred. He was standing for his nightly prayer and a blazing light filled the room, filling him. He forgot everything, even his own body, and was enwrapped in divine light. Then he saw a finer light, higher and more divine. In it stood Symeon the Studite. The experience lasted all night.

He was filled with wonder about this experience, but he was not inwardly strong enough to contain its grace. He quickly forgot his discipline, the experience faded, and he became increasingly involved in his work. All seemed lost, although he sometimes still visited Symeon the Studite.

Seven years passed. Another conversion, which he later attributed only to the prayers of his spiritual father, drove him back to Symeon the Studite, and this time he was admitted to the monastery. Now his real work began.

In a few months, his brother monks could not bear his intensity of devotion and strict practice, so the Abbot had him transferred. Still, the young Symeon remained close to his spiritual father and progressed mightily. In three years, he was a priest and the abbot of his own monastery.

Symeon devoted the next twenty-five years to the monks in his charge, exhorting and teaching them to have their own inner life with God. Symeon's experience of God as Light was repeated and deepened, until he lived in uninterrupted awareness of Christ and the Holy Spirit within himself. He experienced himself as transformed in and by that divine Light. As it had happened to him, he was sure it was for all people. So he championed the necessity of inner experience of God. He insisted that such experiential awareness of Christ should be a prerequisite for all Church leadership.

Of course, this got him in trouble, and in 1005 he resigned his position as abbot to give all his attention to writing, teaching, and defending himself against Church accusations. In 1009 Archbishop Stephen had Symeon exiled. In exile, a local noble gave him land with the ruined church of Saint Marina on it. Symeon and a few disciples rebuilt the church and put up a monastery on this site.

A few years later, Church politics gave him reprieve, and he was offered an archbishopric in reparation. He now lived for the inner life alone, however, and he stayed in his exile-become-retreat, writing and teaching until his death in 1022.

BERNARD OF CLAIRVAUX
(1090-1153)

Bernard was one of those people who seemed to have everything in hand right from the beginning. His family was of nobility, and he himself was handsome, charming, persuasive, and admired by women and authorities alike. He was well educated, and any door he had chosen would have opened for him. He chose the monastery.

Entering at twenty-two, he gave everything to the austere life at Citeaux. He loved it from the beginning, but he was not convinced that the rule there was enough. So he added heavy physical austerities, soaked himself in Scripture and the Fathers, and worked hard. He hardly knew what the chapel looked like, his interior focus was so intense. Renunciation of his own will and everything in the world in favor of interior life with God—this was his way and the way he insisted should be for everyone.

It was said that his efforts were beyond human nature. They were; they were inspired and supported by his interior experience, which, unfortunately for us, he described only indirectly. Nevertheless, he did say that his inner fire was lit in contemplation and that it was from the Spirit within that his work, his writing, and his activity all flowed.

In 1115 he left Citeaux to found an even stricter monastery at Clairvaux, taking with him twelve companions. People streamed to him there from all walks of life, some only to listen, some to stay. Within ten years, the community had grown large enough to found three new monasteries, which themselves sprouted new ones. By the time of Bernard's death, three hundred fifty monasteries had been established under his Cistercian rule.

His personal characteristics seemed universal. He was a skilled administrator, interested in everything; he understood his times and knew art, architecture, and music. Most important, he knew himself and he knew God. Therefore, he knew others. He was a genius, indeed. He would have been a success anywhere. But his lasting impact came from the fact that he strove with all his might to attune his whole being to God—actions, thoughts, aims, hopes, love. He gave all to God alone, full of love. He taught his followers to enjoy God within, and hundreds followed him to God for love alone.

The year 1127 marked a change in Bernard's life. The Spirit sent him out into the world to resolve controversies, to write a rule for the Knights Templar, to handle temporal matters for the Church, to try to resolve papal schisms. He fought hard against people he regarded as heretical. He wrote constantly, even on horseback. He preached everywhere about the Christian life, both interior and external. He urged the Second Crusade into actuality. When it failed, Bernard had to accept the humiliation of people acting in his name for motives lower than his own.

He never hesitated to speak the truth to people in power—kings, popes, archbishops, all came under his attack if they swerved away from God. He demanded holiness from everyone, and amazingly, they listened to him and their behavior was altered.

Through all his activity, his health was never good, having long been broken by his youthful austerities. He was in almost constant pain all his years, but it served to intensify his love for God. His death came at Clairvaux, and his companions said they saw the Blessed Virgin come to welcome him.

HILDEGARD OF BINGEN
(1098-1179)

Born near the Rhine River in today's Germany, Hildegard began to have visions when she was six. She was such an exceptional child that she was given into the care of a hermit attached to a Benedictine double community. Her inner experiences continued, though she said very little to anyone about them. She took her own monastic vows in this cloister, and in 1136 her sisters elected her to be their abbess.

Some five years later, a vision commanded her to write down what she had seen and heard inwardly in order that people could learn from her how to enter the kingdom of God. She obeyed. Her writings first became public when they were read at a Synod in 1147. The bishops were enthusiastic, and she was fully supported by Bernard of Clairvaux. Even the pope encouraged her inner life and her sharing of it.

In the 1140s Hildegard moved her nuns to a new convent at Bingen, away from the men's half of the double community. The abbot was upset with her, and it was years before they could be reconciled. In Bingen, her work flourished.

She wrote much more, even a book on nature and medicine, for she was a healer. She explored questions of sin and virtue as well as the relation of the Creator to the cosmos. She wrote hundreds of letters. She also composed music and lyrics, even a musical morality play (which has been performed in the twentieth century). She commented on the Benedictine Rule, on the gospels, and on the lives of several saints. We even have paintings of some of her visions, though these were supervised by her rather than painted by her hand.

Hildegard founded a second convent. She traveled in response to inner direction, including four trips for preaching. She helped Bernard preach for his Crusade, but especially she cried out for reform in the Church. She challenged clergy and religious to be what they were meant to be, but she did not ignore laypeople, for weren't they all called to be truly Christian?

Her concerns were nearly universal, including care for nature itself and motherly response to the hundreds who sought her for healing and advice.

When she died at eighty-one, those around her saw streams of light from the sky form a cross over her room.

Hildegard had not intended to be so involved in public work. She had begun simply to seek God as a Benedictine. Her writing, travel, and preaching came only when she was commanded to it by her inner visions. Everything she undertook in action flowed directly and exclusively from her interior life with God. Her interior life empowered her to overcome her own shyness, to fulfill her considerable natural abilities, and to speak freely on any subject suggested by the Spirit within.

Although well-known and loved in her own time, she was practically ignored until the twentieth century. Only in the last fifteen or so years has her writing been available in English. Now, however, she is regarded as a prophet, not only to her own time but to ours as well. The breadth of Hildegard's interests and the depth of her inner life speak directly to modern needs.

BONAVENTURE
(1217-1274)

Because Bonaventure is considered the "second founder" of the Franciscans, it is noteworthy that he was born when Francis was bringing the Order to its peak. He never met Francis, who died while Bonaventure was a boy, but felt close to him because his mother's prayers to Francis cured young Bonaventure from an otherwise fatal illness.

In 1234, at age seventeen, Bonaventure began to study at the University of Paris. There he met living Franciscans. Bonaventure arrived as one of the famous professors entered the Franciscan Order and took his university professorship with him. Thus began the intellectual apostolate of the Franciscans, which was to be profoundly furthered by Bonaventure himself.

Nine years later, Bonaventure became a Franciscan and studied theology with great Franciscan theologians. His brilliant mind was not his only fine characteristic. He was known to be humble and always a willing learner. His holiness was acknowledged by all. Profound humility and great intellect found a lovely balance in Bonaventure.

In 1248 he began to lecture at the university and soon became the leader of the Franciscan school there. He was primarily a teacher, though he wrote constantly. In 1257 his confreres elected him minister general of the Order.

Bonaventure's task was to direct the Order in a critical formative period when tensions were high between those who clung to the simplicity of Assisi and those who believed in the intellectual life. Bonaventure found a middle way, urging moderation and simple holiness while encouraging the life of the mind and establishing centers for study. In his view, poverty and learning need not be in conflict if the people who participated sought holiness for love of God.

Other controversies claimed his attention. Clergy were divided, and the mendicant orders and the secular clerics quarreled. Often Bonaventure helped others resolve major disagreements, including their sense of territoriality in Church life.

We know nothing of Bonaventure's interior life except what can be inferred from his prolific and profound writing. There we see that he was more akin to such earlier mystical theologians as Dionysius and Augustine and Bernard than to contemporary philosopher-theologians like his friend Thomas Aquinas, with whom he often debated. If he found the mystics congenial reading, it is likely that his own interior life was rich enough to appreciate them.

Bonaventure's writings have influenced—one could even say formed—Franciscan spirituality through the years. He was able to put into symbol and word what he knew from within, where his own simplicity and love for Christ found new expression through his brilliant mind.

In 1273 Bonaventure was made cardinal bishop, and his immediate task was to help Pope Gregory X prepare for the Second Council of Lyons. It was a reforming Council, especially effective in reconciling the secular clergy with the religious orders.

While at the Council he had helped to build, Bonaventure died and was buried by grieving cardinals and prelates and the pope as well.

MEISTER ECKHART
(1260-1327)

Johannes Eckhart was born to the steward of a knight in Thuringia, the central part of present-day Germany. He came to be called "Meister" (Master), an academic title, and so it has remained. Just as he was controversial in his own time, he is controversial today. Nevertheless, his own life had one goal, one interest, one devotion, one determination: God.

At fifteen or so, he entered the Dominican monastery at Erfurt, studied the required nine years for ordination, and then continued his studies at Cologne. Sometime before 1300, he was elected prior of the monastery at home in Erfurt. About the turn of the century, he was sent by the Order to Paris to dispute with the Franciscans, with whom the Dominicans were in long rivalry. During this time, he received the master's degree.

From then onward, Meister Eckhart rapidly climbed the ladder of position in the Dominican Order. He became Provincial of Saxony in 1303 and four years later Vicar General. In 1313 he returned to teaching in Strasbourg.

As with other holy ones, we know very little about Meister Eckhart's personal life except what we gather from his writing. But he could not have written as he did without a profound, rich interior experience of God. He speaks with the authority of inner knowledge and the brilliance of a good education. He aims always at helping the faithful truly experience God, know him firsthand, love him above all, seek union with him more than anything else in life—as Meister Eckhart himself did. He wants Christians to be thorough, holy, and joyful.

Eckhart's preaching and teaching included not only the intellectual sophisticates but also the ordinary people of a parish and those who wrote to him from all over Europe. He was in great demand as a spiritual guide by laypeople and especially by the nuns whom it was his task to teach.

The fact that he believed that God was for any social class and any level of education (or lack of it) meant that he preached and wrote his convictions and the results of his inner experience to all—and in German dialect, not only in Latin. That meant that the highest ideas could be offered to all. This did not sit well with some Church authorities.

This freedom to preach to all—coupled with the politico/religious machinations endemic in the Middle Ages—got Meister Eckhart in trouble. Complaints went to the authorities that Eckhart's preaching could be harmfully misunderstood by the uneducated. He was charged with heresy. He died in the midst of his own defense. Certain of his ideas were condemned a few weeks later on the grounds that they could lead people into error, something he himself would never have wished to do.

Modern scholars and theologians have "reopened the case" on Meister Eckhart in a way, searching into the processes and the documents of the trial. They conclude that Eckhart taught nothing that had not been taught by the early Church Fathers. Indeed, some points that seemed the worst to Church authorities in the Middle Ages can be found in Augustine as well. What Meister Eckhart did was speak bluntly from his own interior experience and teach mystical principles to all who would listen. That was not to his own advantage in a time when spiritual hungers were running high and Church authorities felt quite threatened by them.

THE AUTHOR OF THE CLOUD OF UNKNOWING
(Late Fourteenth Century)

The unwelcome fact is that the name of the author of this loved work, so much used over the centuries, is unknown. The book was written in English, and linguists point to the area of the northeast Midlands of Britain as its most likely geographic origin. By cross references, we can be sure that it was written in the late 1300s, making the author a contemporary (among our authors in this selection) of Catherine of Siena, Birgitta of Sweden, and Julian of Norwich.

Speculation about the author has included the probability that he was a priest, a religious, and a spiritual director. Others prefer to speculate that this writer was a woman and therefore preferred the anonymity that has remained to this day. But in spite of these speculations, we know nothing personal about the author.

The writing reflects considerable knowledge of earlier mystical theologians, referring to some of them by name and reflecting the thought of others. Whoever the author was, he or she was a student of mystical theology. In the fourteenth century, this would usually point to formal theological training.

The writer wrote other treatises as well, including the most mature work, called *The Book of Privy Counseling* ("privy" means private or personal), offered to a directee, perhaps, well along on the contemplative path.

Anonymity frustrates the modern reader. We want to know individual names and traits. We value the individual identity more than almost anything else. But it was not always thus in every culture nor in every individual. For this author, personal individuality was far less important than the content of the writing, and neither was as important as the reality of a life fully lived in "naked love" for God.

Even more than that, to enjoy union with God is, for this writer, to be lost in God in a certain sense. The "cloud" that covers memories and thoughts and all such occupations ultimately covers the individual also, until only God remains. It was perhaps in this spirit of "losing one's life to save it," as Jesus said, that the author of *The Cloud of Unknowing* has chosen to be anonymous forever except in the heart of God.

BIRGITTA OF SWEDEN
(1302-1373)

Birgitta came of nobility and was close to aristocratic society the first half of her life. She was raised in a loving Christian family. At fourteen, as was customary, she married. She and her husband later joined the Franciscan Third Order, indicating their mutual dedication to Christian life. They had eight children. Birgitta's responsibility included, for several years, management of the royal court in Stockholm. So she can truly be called a working mother!

Her husband died in 1344 after twenty-eight years of happy married life, for they loved not only God but each other as well. Insofar as they could decide their own lifestyle, with the court obligations they bore, they lived frugally and practiced a certain asceticism.

When her husband died, Birgitta began a secluded life of prayer and self-denial under a wise spiritual director, Master Matthias. Her mystical life began during this time, and God gave her her first revelations. These were to increase with time.

As she obeyed instructions in her revelations, she began to denounce the values currently in vogue in the Swedish court. She also laid plans for a new religious Order, organized as it had been revealed to her: a double Order of nuns, lay Brothers, and priests under the overall direction of an abbess.

As her revelations continued and her life changed in obedient response, she kept close by her always a respected priest as spiritual director. Because she was astounded that God would reveal greatness to and through a woman, she always sought corroboration of her visions from other people of wisdom and experience.

She began to write, denouncing in her books the corruptions in the Church and begging for reform and return to real Christian principles. She especially warned of Church splits, which were endemic in the fourteenth century. The rulers of Europe also were not exempt from her attacks for their worldliness and injustice. Naturally, they were not fond of her. But her inner life sustained her and urged her on.

She went to Rome in 1349 and thereafter was a persistent pilgrim, traveling at inner promptings to intervene in social affairs as the Spirit deemed her obedient voice to be needed.

In 1370 her new Order was approved by Pope Urban VI, an approval that implied appreciation of her mission and of the rightness of her inner life and direction.

Soon after, divine instruction sent her to the Holy Land, where her visions centered around the life of Christ and the Blessed Virgin. But while there, she became ill.

Returning to Rome, she died in July 1373. A year later, her body was moved to the motherhouse of her new Order in Sweden.

She was well-known during her lifetime and highly controversial. The well-placed often opposed her, and many of her prophetic warnings were never heeded. But more ordinary people who sought God found in her example and her writings both inspiration and concrete help.

JULIAN OF NORWICH
(1342-not before 1413)

Of "Mother" Julian, little biographical can be said. We simply do not have information.

In her book, *Showings,* we are told the date of her visions and her age at the time (thirty-one), so we know her year of birth. She is mentioned in another writer's manuscript as still living in 1413, so she died sometime after that.

We know that at the time of her writings, she was an anchoress in a cell attached to the church of Saint Julian at Carrow in Norwich, England. As was customary, she assumed the name of the church when she took her vow never to leave this cell and to spend her life in prayer and counseling those who came to her.

We do not know her given name, her family background, whether she was unmarried or a widow, or whether she had children. She writes nothing about the catastrophic events of her times (the Black Death and many wars, some in her own town), though she shows a deep sensitivity to human sufferings and challenges God to explain them. Whether she was ever a member of a religious Order is unknown.

In 1373—and we don't know whether she was yet an anchoress—Julian became deathly ill. She writes that all her life she had prayed to share in Christ's passion. Those around her, and indeed she herself, believed she was dying. In the midst of this extremity, she had a series of intense, vivid, and detailed visions: sixteen visions in several hours' time. When these visions ceased, her body was well on its way to being wholly healed.

Soon after, she wrote down her visions and as much of their meaning as she understood. She pondered them and prayed over them for the rest of her life. Some twenty years later, she wrote about them again, now including all the meanings that had been given to her in that time. Her writings show familiarity with other mystical and doctrinal treatises and suggest that she was a woman of some education—not usual for her century but not unheard of either.

Julian speaks freely of her interior spiritual experiences but only insofar as she judges them to be useful for other people's progress in spiritual life. She gives no personal details that would satisfy our twentieth-century curiosity. Besides this spiritual intimacy, her work is marked by a deep awareness of God's love, Christ's love for every single human being. Her profound teachings are meant to encourage others and draw them toward the experience of the indwelling Trinity which she knew.

She is also known for writing delicately and strongly of the Motherhood of God and of Jesus to all people.

Perhaps the most famous sentence in all her work, translated from the Middle English in which Julian wrote, is this: *All things shall be well, and all things shall be well, and all manner of things shall be exceedingly well!*

CATHERINE OF SIENA
(1347-1380)

Catherine's spirit and life draw enthusiastic followers even today, for it was only in 1970 that she was given the title Doctor of the Church.

Born in the year the Black Plague came to Europe, Catherine lived in a century of terror caused by illness and death, wars, and a splintering Church. She was twenty-fourth of twenty-five children born to a comfortable family, beloved of all and full of devotion to God. Early in life she vowed virginity and at fifteen refused to marry—to her parents' consternation. At eighteen she received the Dominican habit of the "Mantellate," women who lived in their homes and served God and the sick and poor.

But Catherine took to her room and did not leave it for three years, except for Mass. Her interior, visionary life became strong during this period, and she experienced "mystical marriage" to Christ at twenty-one. With that, her inner foundation was completed, and the Lord commanded her to leave her solitude and give her life in service.

It was not Catherine's wish, but her strength had long been in obedience. From this time on, stories about her show a wonderful caretaker of all who needed her—the sick, the poor, those who wanted to be taught. She even held the head of a young man she had visited in prison while he was beheaded. She drew people in dozens and showed them how to live close to God. She dictated hundreds of letters and composed a book, *The Dialogue,* putting her understandings in the form of a conversation with God.

She ate almost nothing except the consecrated host and slept very little. In the midst of all this activity, her inner experiences with God continued. External events no longer determined her interior vitality. Her teachings and her impact on people sprang only from her intense inner life with Christ.

The Church and the papacy were in terrible crisis in the fourteenth century. Catherine jumped into the battles. Her devotion to the truth was her standard for all—individuals, situations, city-states, the

Church, and even the pope. She traveled as propelled by the inner Word, a great deal for a young woman of her time. She saved the countryside from the ravages of mercenary soldiers, preached a Crusade, clamored for the reform of the clergy, and worked tirelessly for the pope's return to Rome from Avignon.

Deeply involved in social questions that would never be clearly right or wrong, she gave herself totally to support whatever she saw as right. Her devotion to God's cause never hesitated. If she was naive and if she seemed to court death itself, it must be said she would not have objected to martyrdom.

One of Catherine's lasting causes was unity in the Church, and to this she gave enormous energy. Eventually, the pope did return to Rome. When later he summoned Catherine, she went, counseling him and others in an attempt to keep the Church from splintering.

Her body finally collapsed under all this ill treatment. For the last four months of her life, she could not even take water. Until her legs would no longer carry her, she struggled daily to Mass and prayed there, often in ecstasy, until evening. Catherine died in Rome at the age of thirty-three.

ANGELUS SILESIUS
(1624-1677)

His given name was Johannes Scheffler. He was born during the religious strife known as the Thirty Years' War, when Protestants and Catholics were killing one another all over Europe. Governments took sides, and one's religion was either legal or illegal, depending largely on the local nobility's preference and power. Horrors and hatreds filled that period, yet Scheffler's verses, collected in *The Cherubinic Wanderer,* exude peace and joy in God.

Scheffler's Lutheran parents were wealthy enough that, even though they died in his youth, he was able to study medicine and philosophy. Born in Poland, he studied in France, Italy, and Holland, receiving degrees in both his chosen fields. But his adulthood was dogged by the controversies of the Counter Reformation, a Catholic movement that attempted—often with violence—to re-Catholicize areas of Europe that had become predominantly Protestant.

His first known encounter with the conflict was when he attempted to get his early mystical verses published but was refused by the Lutheran censor, even though he himself was Lutheran. At the same time, he was reading the *Exercises of Saint Ignatius* and began a spiritual diary. We do not know for sure what intensified an existing interest in Catholicism, but less than a year later, Johannes Scheffler became Roman Catholic and took the name Angelus Silesius. Later he was to become a priest, some say a Franciscan, although he never seems to have lived in community.

Since the new Catholic was already well known in his area as a doctor and writer, the Catholic vicar influenced him to become a writer for the Catholic cause, while at the same time allowing him to publish what he had already written. Both events must have meant a great deal to Angelus. As a result, he became one of the strongest, most vitriolic of writers against the Protestants and for the Catholics.

While today we would look askance at that intolerance and angry activity, in his own time, it was undoubtedly regarded as high virtue.

He was, after all, serving the cause of the Church as it wanted him to in a time of violent religionism.

More importantly for us, amid all this external furor, Angelus was living a thorough Christian life. In spite of his wealth, he practiced considerable asceticism. He served the poor, especially mentoring their children. He gave alms freely. He cared for the sick and helped the orphans. He donated much to organizations devoted to religious purposes, in the end giving away most of his inheritance. Of his inner life, we know little except what we glean from his verses. They reveal a spirit deeply at one with God, in mutual love and awareness.

Eventually, Angelus' health broke under the stresses of his involvement in conflicts for the sake of his chosen Church. His writings addressing those conflicts have little interest today, except to historians of the period. Two years before he died, however, his mystical verses entered their second edition, an indication of their popularity among the people. These verses speak to us today as well, as in them he penetrates many aspects of the deification in Christ open to Christians. Short and pungent, Angelus' verses pierce our understanding and carry us a little along the way to God that he himself must have gone to write them.

Bibliography

Angelus Silesius: The Cherubinic Wanderer, translated by Maria Shrady. New York: Paulist Press, 1986.

Bernard of Clairvaux, translated by G.R. Evans. New York: Paulist Press, 1987.

Birgitta of Sweden, edited by Marguerite Tjader Harris. New York: Paulist Press, 1990.

Bonaventure, translated by Ewert Cousins. New York: Paulist Press, 1978.

Catherine of Siena: The Dialogue, translated by Suzanne Noffke, O.P. New York: Paulist Press, 1980.

The Cloud of Unknowing, edited by William Johnston. Garden City, NY: Doubleday Image, 1973.

Evagrius Ponticus: The Praktikos and Chapters on Prayer, translated by John Eudes Bamberger, O.C.S.O. Kalamazoo, MI: Cistercian Publications, 1978.

Fox, Matthew. *Illuminations of Hildegard of Bingen.* Santa Fe, NM: Bear and Company, 1985.

From Glory to Glory, translated and edited by Herbert Musurillo, S.J. Crestwood, NY: St. Vladimir's Seminary Press, 1979.

Gregory of Nyssa, *The Life of Moses,* translated by Abraham Malherbe and Everett Ferguson. New York: Paulist Press, 1978.

Hildegard's Scivias, edited by Bruce Hozeski. Santa Fe, NM: Bear and Company, 1986.

Jantzen, Grace M. *Julian of Norwich.* New York: Paulist Press, 1988.

Light From Light: An Anthology of Christian Mysticism, edited by Louis Dupre and James A. Wiseman, O.S.B. New York: Paulist Press, 1988.

Maximus the Confessor, translated by George C. Berthold. New York: Paulist Press, 1985.

Meister Eckhart, translated by Raymond B. Blakney. New York: Harper and Brothers, 1941.

Meister Eckhart: The Essential Sermons, Commentaries, Treatises and Defense, translated by Edmund Colledge, O.S.A., and Bernard McGinn. New York: Paulist Press, 1981.

Nomura, Yushi. *Desert Wisdom.* Garden City, NY: Doubleday, 1982.

The Philokalia, Volume Two, translated and edited by G.E.H. Palmer, Philip Sherrard, and Kallistos Ware. Winchester, MA: Faber and Faber, Inc., 1986.

Sayings of the Desert Fathers, translated by Benedicta Ward, SLG. Kalamazoo, MI: Cistercian Publications, 1978.

Symeon the New Theologian: The Discourses, translated by C.J. deCatanzaro. New York: Paulist Press, 1980.

Writings from the Philokalia on the Prayer of the Heart, translated by E. Kadloubovsky and G.E.H. Palmer. London: Faber and Faber Ltd., 1951.